25 CYCLE ROUTES

EDINBURGH
AND
LOTHIAN

Derek Purdy
and
Erl B. Wilkie

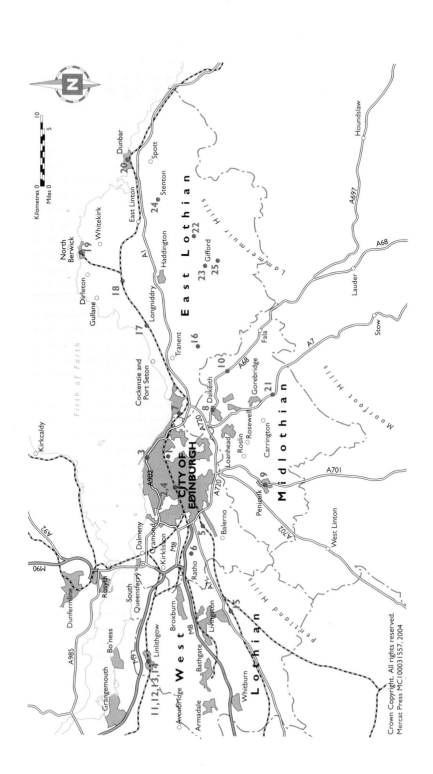

25 CYCLE ROUTES

EDINBURGH
AND
LOTHIAN

**Derek Purdy
and
Erl B. Wilkie**

With a Foreword by CTC

MERCAT PRESS

First edition by Derek Purdy published in 1996 by HMSO
Second edition by Erl Wilkie published in 2004 by Mercat Press
at 10 Coates Crescent, Edinburgh EH3 7AL
www.mercatpress.com

ISBN: 1 84183 060 7

Also available in this series:
25 Cycle Routes—In and Around Glasgow
25 Cycle Routes—Stirling and the Trossachs
25 Cycle Routes—Kingdom of Fife
25 Cycle Routes—Argyll and Bute

Acknowledgements

Erl Wilkie wishes to thank Spokes, the Lothian Cycle Campaign,
whose detailed cycle maps of the area were an invaluable aid in
assessing the routes. In particular he is grateful to Ian Maxwell of
Spokes who scanned the text for inaccuracies in the description of
the routes. Matthew Simpson of the City of Edinburgh Council and
Graeme Malcolm of West Lothian Council also scrutinised some
routes within their areas, and for this also deserve my thanks; as do
Graeme Pate and Tom A'hara—the first helped with the index and
the second kept the technology working.

A special thanks goes to Dougie Brown of 'Freewheelin', the bicycle
shop in Penicuik, who helped me out on a day when I had problems
with my own bike. This man's ability to help others is boundless, and
he is particularly known for the work he does to help the young
people of the area.

All photographs Erl B. Wilkie

CONTENTS

FOREWORD BY CTC

Cycling is healthy, environmentally-friendly—and above all fun! Travel at your own pace, meet people along the way and experience the real country. Explore parts of the country that you didn't know existed—and improve your fitness at the same time! Cycling is good for you, so go by bike, and you'll feel a whole lot better for it.

Safety considerations and equipment needed

• Before you go cycling, check your bike thoroughly for broken, worn and/or loose parts. In particular, check for worn tyres and broken/loose spokes. Ensure that both brakes and the gear system are working well, with the chain lightly oiled and running smoothly. If in doubt your local bike shop will advise you further. Better to fix things now, than to spoil your ride later.

• Carry a cycle lock and key, and a small tool kit (spare inner tube, tyre levers, small adjustable spanner, puncture repair outfit, pump and Allen keys if your bike needs them).

• If you are really loading up for a big adventure your luggage should be on the bike not your back. A rear carrying rack is useful. Ideally pack everything into plastic bags inside a saddlebag or panniers properly secured to this rack. Check your load is balanced, and the weight doesn't affect the steering/handling of the bike. If you prefer to travel light you can fit most things into a bumbag.

• Always carry food and water/liquid. Cyclists are advised to drink little and often.

• Comfortable clothing is essential. For colder days wear two or three layers: you can take them off once you've warmed up and put them on if you cool off. Wet-weather gear is useful if you've got the space to carry it. For hot weather don't forget your sun cream and shades.

METRIC MEASUREMENTS

At the beginning of each route, the distance is given in miles and kilometres. Within the text, all measurements are metric for simplicity (and indeed our Ordnance Survey maps are now all metric). However, it was felt that a conversion table might be useful to those readers who, like the author, still tend to think in miles.

The basic statistic to remember is that one kilometre is five-eighths of a mile. Half a mile is equivalent to 800 metres and a quarter-mile is 400 metres. Below that distance, yards and metres are little different in practical terms.

km	miles
1	0.625
1.6	1
2	1.25
3	1.875
3.2	2
4	2.5
4.8	3
5	3.125
6	3.75
6.4	4
7	4.375
8	5
9	5.625
10	6.25
16	10

- You don't have to wear specialist cycle clothing to enjoy cycling. Padded shorts, gloves, cycling shoes, cycle helmets and much more can be purchased at cycle shops if you are interested. NB It is not compulsory to wear a helmet, and the choice is yours. CTC can provide further information on helmets if needed.

- Check your riding position is comfortable. Saddle height: when seated, place your heel on the pedal when it is at its lowest point. Your leg should be straight, and your knee just off the locked position. On the subject of riding comfort, many bikes are supplied with saddles designed for men (long and narrow). Women may prefer to sit on a saddle designed for women (shorter and wider at the back). These are available from bike shops.

- There is some useful information for cyclists in the *Highway Code*. This is available from garages, bookshops and may be found in your library.

- If you think that you may be cycling when it is dark, you will need to fit front and rear lights. (This is a legal requirement.) Lights and reflectors/reflective clothing are also useful in bad weather conditions.

- In the event of an accident, it is advisable to note the time and place of the incident, the names and addresses of those involved, details of their insurance company, and vehicle registration numbers and details of any witnesses. In the event of injury or damage, report the incident to the police immediately.

 For further information about cycling...

CTC (Cyclists' Touring Club) is Britain's largest cycling organisation, and can provide a wealth of information and advice about all aspects of cycling. CTC works on behalf of all cyclists to promote cycling and to protect cyclists' interests.

Membership includes free third-party insurance, legal aid, touring and technical information, a bi-monthly magazine and a cyclists' handbook.

For further details contact CTC at: Cotterell House, 69 Meadrow, Godalming, Surrey GU7 3HS; or telephone 0870 8730060, fax 0870 8730064; or e-mail *cycling@ctc.org.uk*; or visit the website: *www.ctc.org.uk*.

INTRODUCTION

The second edition of this guide still embraces the two principal philosophies of the first edition. The first is to encourage those who are new to cycling and those who have not ridden a bike for a long time, or those who think they might like cycling, to go out and do it. Secondly, to get you into virtually every corner of Lothian. The second edition has therefore gone into more detail about the points of interest on the way around each route, and highlights the many places of historical interest in this fascinating part of Scotland. It has also looked at how the cycle routes can be made accessible for the largest number of people who wish to use them. Therefore, 12 of the routes start and end at railway stations and 3 more are easily accessed from Edinburgh Waverley Station. Where there is no railway in the vicinity of the route it starts at a convenient car park. The majority of the routes, 23 out of the 25, have now been made circular, and to achieve this, four completely new routes have been added. There are short routes, most of which are predominantly traffic-free, railway path routes which are totally devoid of steep gradients and canal routes which are also completely flat but invariably have a hilly little road to complement them. At the other end of the cycling scale there is a ride to the highest tarmac road in Lothian. Start small and work your way up! The routes are all enjoyable if you take your time.

The three counties of East, Mid and West Lothian, together with the City of Edinburgh, form the historical region known as Lothian. It is a diverse, interesting and beautiful area which has lots to offer, from ranges of hills to a varied coastline and with everything in between. The four council authorities have created many cycle facilities, and it is only right that they should be a main feature in a guide of this type. They are arguably some of the best in the country.

Where off-road routes have been used they have been checked out as well as possible to ascertain the right of access. However, sometimes it is not clear if a stretch of path is or is not a right of way, as many in Scotland are informal. Though the recent government legislation on access to the countryside does now help to clarify this situation, in all cases the responsibility for checking lies with the individual who is cycling on any path or stretch of land. Remember, there is a law of trespass in Scotland, and although one cannot be prosecuted for crossing private land one can be sued for damage.

On occasion some of the routes use A and B class roads, but I have avoided using very busy roads except when they are an unavoidable short link with much quieter stretches of road. I feel if these roads are used properly and with care they should not cause any problems and should not detract from the enjoyment of the overall route. However, the reader must make his or her own judgement about safety depending on the circumstances prevailing at the time. If in doubt do not attempt it!

I hope you will enjoy these routes which pass through a very varied terrain.

SPOKES

Since 1977, SPOKES has been campaigning to promote cycling and improve conditions for cyclists in Lothian. Many of the cycle path routes described in this book resulted from suggestions by SPOKES and other local cycling organisations, and some of the links were constructed by campaign volunteers.

SPOKES is a non-party-political voluntary organisation with around 1,000 members throughout Lothian and beyond. Members get regular news about campaign activities, including monthly cycle rides and stalls at events. They are kept in touch with local transport and planning developments.

Four cycle maps are published by SPOKES, covering Edinburgh, East Lothian, Midlothian and West Lothian. They show cycle paths, quiet roads, gradients and other features important to cyclists. Priced £4.95 each, they can be obtained from cycle shops and bookshops throughout the area, or from the spokes web site at *www.spokes.org.uk*.

For further information contact SPOKES on 0131 313 2114 or email spokes@spokes.org.uk

CYCLING SCOTLAND

Cycling Scotland's goal is to present cycling as a practical, attractive and accessible lifestyle option. It will assist in achieving an increase in cycle use in line with the Government's National Cycling Strategy targets of a quadrupling of 1996 figures by 2012. An increase in cycle use in Scotland will be of advantage to more than just those who cycle. Shorter journey times, decreased pressure on the road network, less demand on the health service and a healthier, more pleasant environment will benefit the whole nation.

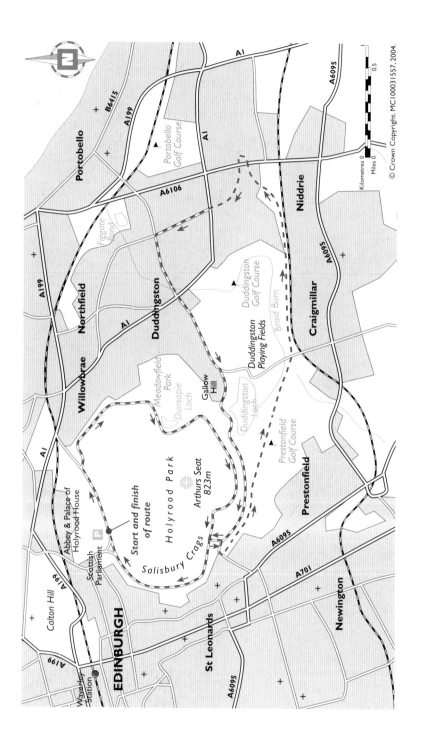

HOLYROOD PARK AND THE INNOCENT RAILWAY

The elevated parts of Holyrood Park dominate Edinburgh. The line of Salisbury Crags and the huge mound of Arthur's Seat can be seen for miles around. At 251 m the Seat is less than 1,000 feet high, but to the north there is nothing higher until you are halfway across Fife. A road circumnavigates the hill providing a spectacular tour, and by linking this to the Innocent Railway path you have the ingredients of a very interesting ride.

Start at the car park just off Queen's Drive next to the Palace of Holyrood House, the principal home of the monarch in Scotland. Carry on past the diminutive, but very popular St Margaret's Loch and climb the hill away from Meadowbank towards Dunsapie Loch. It is a one-way system. The ascent is steep and sustained for well over a kilometre, easing only on the approach to Dunsapie Loch, but there is plenty to see and the effort is well worth it. The little loch is a windy spot, but despite this swans have nested here and many birds use it as a feeding ground. The ride now takes on a truly high-level and exposed feel. The road is set against rock walls above Samson's Ribs with unimpeded views to the south and west. Way down below you can see the line of the railway path beyond Duddingston Loch.

Serious effort over, the road sweeps down to the roundabout at Salisbury Crags where you turn left, then right to St Leonard's.

Salisbury Crags appealed strongly to the eighteenth-century admirers of the picturesque, but are no less attractive today. The early visitors claimed they were virtually unscalable, but

INFORMATION

Distance: 12 km (7.5 miles). Circular route.

Map: OS Landranger, sheet 66 and Spokes Edinburgh Cycle Map.

Start and finish: Holyrood car park, Holyrood Park.

Terrain: Park roads, cycle path and quiet streets. Steep climb up Queen's Drive/Arthur's Seat. The rest is generally flat with some short hills.

Refreshments: Sheep's Heid, Duddingston.

The Bonnie Wells o' Wearle

Arthur's Seat

modern-day rock climbers find them a great lure, so much so that the Park's Police spend a fair bit of energy attempting to discourage them.

It is quite hard to imagine that they were once heavily quarried. In the early nineteenth century the removal of rock was apparently hardly noticeable, but unemployment and severe distress after the Napoleonic wars led to the creation of a fund to employ out-of-work shawl-weavers and others to clear the ground and make a new path at the foot of the crags. This became known as the Radical Road, as most of the destitute were, or were believed to be, supporters of the principles of the French Revolution. Unfortunately its creation caused bother for one Scottish aristocrat, Lord Haddington, hereditary Keeper of the King's Park. He had the stone quarried and sold for his own profit, most of it going to the town council, but when the citizens found out how the Keeper had been keeping the park, an action was commenced against him, which ended twelve years later when the House of Lords decreed that no more stone was to be quarried, and the crags were saved.

Ride across the bridge into Holyrood Park Road, which is actually the tunnel you are about to use. Turn right into East Parkside then right again at the blue cycleway sign, through the courtyard of the new housing estate and on into the tunnel.

The tunnel was created for the Edinburgh and Dalkeith Railway, one of the oldest railways built in Scotland and the first to carry passengers. It was planned and built between 1826 and 1831 by Edinburgh engineer James Jardine at a cost of £80,000, the biggest single expenditure being for the tunnel which had to be driven under part of Arthur's Seat.

The name 'The Innocent Railway' was first applied as a jibe, for although, at the time of its opening, steam railways did exist in other parts of the country, none did in Scotland. This railway was driven by horse power and it was first referred to as 'innocent' by Doctor James Chalmers because of its simplicity—there were no intermediate stations, passengers being able to join or alight at will along its length. Later this name was to signal its unique record in being completely accident-free compared to the steam-driven railways in other areas, where serious accidents were a frequent event.

Sustrans national cycle signing on the Innocent Railway

Steam was used however in the tunnel under Arthur's Seat where, because of the steep gradient of 1 in 30, horse power was not adequate. For the first three years the railway was used exclusively for the movement of coal from the pits close by in Midlothian, but a contractor called Fox had the idea of capitalising on this little railway as a novelty to the people of the surrounding district. For carriages he used flat trucks without sides. In each he managed to carry 40 people and in his first year made a net a profit of four thousand pounds. In the years that followed, this railway provided thousands of people with a cheap link to and from the city of Edinburgh, and in the first four years of operation it carried over a million passengers.

Today the route through the tunnel may seem like a daunting task to many cyclists, but in fact in my few journeys through it I have never come across any circumstances which gave me any cause for concern, and the well-lit tunnel itself is kept clean, free of litter and broken glass.

After emerging from the tunnel on the other side the way continues past Arthur's Seat. Between this and the cycle route are the Bonnie Wells o' Wearie, close to Duddingston Loch, which were immortalised in the song of

The Palace of Holyrood House

the same name. It was here on 18 September 1745 that Charles Edward Stewart had his troops breach the wall and march into the King's Park. The Young Pretender then rode on to St Anthony's Well, from where he saw, for the first time, the house of his ancestors, the Palace of Holyrood. A few days later he led his soldiers into battle against the opposing Royal army commanded by Lieutenant-General Sir John Cope. The two armies met at Prestonpans, the result being another resounding victory for the Prince and his army of Highlanders.

The area adjacent to the cycleway is, today, part of the Duddingston Nature Reserve, which supports large numbers of wild birds of many species. The cycleway takes you past two golf courses: first, to the south, is Prestonfield Golf Club with its championship course, once the venue for many prestigious golf tournaments. Then on the north side is Duddingston Golf Course.

After passing the golf courses, this clearly defined cycle path goes on uninterrupted through Jewel Park to Duddingston Park South. Here turn left into Mountcastle Drive South. Carry on along this road to the junction with Duddingston Road and turn left.

Follow this road until it becomes Duddingston Road West which joins the Causeway. Here the ancient Duddingston Village is only a few metres to the right.

Duddingston Kirk

Duddingston Village has been in existence in some form or other since the Roman occupation. The name seems to be derived from the Saxon family name Dodin; the earliest known spelling, from the eighth century, is Dodinstun, meaning the land belonging to Dodin. This Saxon family was clearly a very powerful one, because there is considerable evidence that they were signatories of various charters up to the reign of Malcolm IV.

A church was built by the monks of Kelso on the shore of Duddingston Loch in 1143, and some of this original structure still survives today as part of Duddingston Parish Church.

Today Duddingston still maintains its picturesque village character, with its main street, the Causeway, running through it, and its old inn, The Sheep Heid, which was said to have been frequented by James VI before he went to live in London.

After passing Duddingston Village you join the road around Holyrood Park with Duddingston Loch on the left. Follow this road all the way around to join Queen's Drive once again, but this time turn left and head towards the Palace where the route began.

Sheep Heid pub

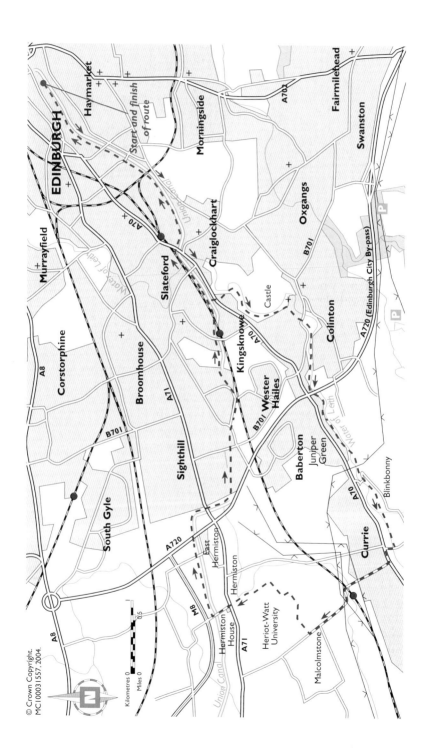

© Crown Copyright.
MC100031557. 2004.

CITY CANAL AND NATIONAL CYCLE ROUTE TO CURRIE

This is the ultimate starter route for young and old alike. Parents might have reservations about taking their children along a canal towpath, which by its very nature has water on one side, but be reassured—the condition of the path is good, there is a grass verge between the edge of the riding surface and the water which in most places is higher than the towpath, and if you dismount to pass under bridges and walk across the Slateford aqueduct there will be no problem. It is usually the parents who are weaving about trying to keep up with flying children! This ride abounds in interest. The canal is a shared leisure facility in a major way. Obviously you will meet people walking, but you will also see oarsmen from more than one club sculling at quite impressive speeds on the short straights, and fishermen too, always after the big pike that is alleged to dwell therein. Be considerate and courteous. You will find others, particularly pedestrians, are extremely so. Return the compliment, and do not be afraid to dismount.

The Union Canal was, compared to other British canals, a latecomer. Work was started in March 1818 after many years of planning, and it finally opened in January 1822. The canal was first envisaged as a cheap method of transporting coal to Edinburgh. The idea had been shown to work by the Forth and Clyde Canal, which had been in operation since 1790, being used to transport coal and other raw materials cheaply and in great bulk to Glasgow. Hugh Baird, the resident engineer of the

INFORMATION

Distance: 21 km (13.2 miles). Circular route.

Start and finish: Harrison Park, North Merchiston, Edinburgh.

Map: OS Landranger 66 and Spokes Edinburgh Cycle Map.

Terrain: Canal towpath, cycle path and quiet suburban streets. Flat city route.

Refreshments: Places in Slateford and Currie.

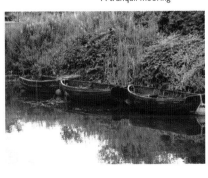

A tranquil mooring

Canal boats

Forth and Clyde Canal, was asked to devise the further route for the proposed canal, with Thomas Telford being consulted on the construction of the aqueducts.

Baird's plan was to construct the canal from Port Hopetoun, which stood where the film theatre on Lothian Road is today. It was to be built along the 240 foot (73 m) contour, entering the Forth and Clyde Canal at a much lower level through a series of locks at Camelon near Falkirk. Cutting the canal along a single contour line avoided the use of locks until it joined the Forth and Clyde Canal, and although this made the route longer in distance, the journey time was faster.

Once the Canal opened in 1822, it enjoyed brief but considerable popularity as a transporter of passengers, with as many as 200,000 people using it in 1836. However, the Glasgow to Edinburgh Railway was opened in 1842, and with the advent of this faster mode of transportation the popularity of the canal dwindled very quickly. However, thanks to its beautiful surroundings, for some further considerable time it was enjoyed as a leisure resource by many people, with pleasure boats plying its length.

In 1921 the canal was shortened by the closure of Port Hopetoun and Port Hamilton, and then closed to navigation, by act of Parliament, in 1965.

The canal starts today in Fountainbridge, just before Gilmore Park, and within a very short distance the traveller passes Leamington Road lifting bridge. This unique electrically operated lifting bridge was moved to its present location from Fountainbridge Road, in 1922, after Ports Hopetoun and Hamilton were closed.

Although at this point it is only a stone's throw from the heart of the city, the canal is teeming with many varieties of wild life. Within 200m you will see breeding pairs of swans, ducks and moorhens, all nesting in the reeds and on the bank opposite the tow path.

The canal runs west past the Edinburgh Canal Society's Boat House, on the opposite bank at Ashley Terrace, and then continues a short distance to Meggetland where Boroughmuir Rugby Club, one of Edinburgh's consistent premiership league clubs, have their playing fields.

Edinburgh Canal Society Boat House

On now to Slateford, where the first two of the many aqueducts are located. The first is known as Prince Charlie's aqueduct. This is a fairly modern structure, having been rebuilt in 1937 when Slateford Road was widened. The reason for the name is that Bonnie Prince Charlie is thought to have stayed at Graysmill Farm House the night before he and his army of Highlanders entered Edinburgh in 1745. This farm house stood near where today Inglis Green Road joins Slateford Road. The second aqueduct at Slateford is Slateford Viaduct, the first of the three large multi-span structures built as part of the original canal.

After Slateford aqueduct, carry on along the tow path for about 500m to where a sign points you south towards Sustrans National Cycle Route 75 to Glasgow. Take the route in this direction as it meanders along the banks of the Water of Leith.

From here it makes its route through a very beautiful and spectacular gorge known as Colinton Dell, emerges on to the now disused Slateford to Balerno branch railway line, and follows the line through the 300-yard-long

Leamington lift bridge

railway tunnel into Colinton village.

The village of Colinton has a recorded history as far back as 1095 when Ethelred, second son of Malcolm Canmore gifted the lands known as Halis to the church of the Holy Trinity in Dunfermline. The village has clustered around Colinton Parish Church and church-yard for many hundreds of years. Here a 'mort safe'—a barred grave enclosure—can still be seen, a chilling reminder of the days when grave robbery was common. Robert Louis Stevenson spent many of his boyhood days here at the manse where his maternal grand-father, the Reverend Lewis Balfour, was minister. The walkway now goes through Spylaw Park, and after going under the huge road bridge which takes the City of Edinburgh Bypass high across the river valley, it continues into the adjoining villages of Juniper Green and Currie, which both have a long milling history. From as far back as the sixteenth century flax, snuff, paper and grain were produced here.

The village of Currie is situated entirely on the other side of Lanark Road, and the footpath, which now keeps to the south side of the river, is still surrounded by picturesque woodland. The route does, however, pass Currie Kirk, which in the thirteenth century was dedicated to St Kentigern or Mungo, the patron saint of Glasgow. The present kirk dates from 1785.

At this point take the access up on to Kirkgate and turn right; soon you will join the busy Lanark Road and turn left. Don't despair, because you are only on this road for some 200m before turning right once again, onto Curriehill Road. Carry on along this road for over 2 km to Avenue West, where you turn right. Follow this as it becomes The Avenue to the T-junction at Boundary Road, and turn left here. Continue to where the road turns about 90 degrees, and here you will find the entrance to a cycle route. A short stretch along this soon takes you to the A71 which you cross, with care, to Hermiston House Road. Soon you cross the canal. Once on the other

New canal at Wester Hailes

side, take the access road down on to the towpath and carry on in an easterly direction back towards Edinburgh. Soon the Scott Russell Aqueduct is reached. This is a new structure which carries the canal over the Edinburgh City Bypass. Once past this the canal soon takes on a different appearance as the Millennium Link is reached. This new canal was constructed to join the existing sections together once again. When the canal was closed in the 1960s the water was taken through a buried culvert. Now, however, because of this new link and the Falkirk Wheel in Falkirk the canal is now once again navigable from Edinburgh to the River Clyde at Bowling.

Once you are back on the original canal, Slateford Aqueduct is soon reached, and from here you retrace the outgoing route back to Fountainbridge.

You mean we're in a city?

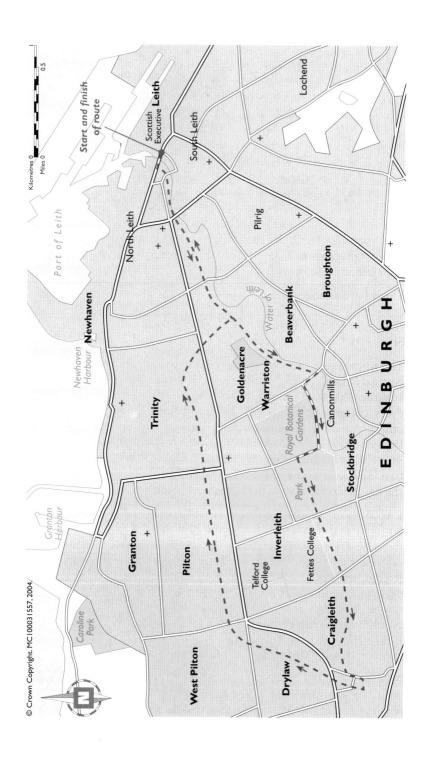

© Crown Copyright. MCI0003I557, 2004.

LEITH AND INVERLEITH

This route utilises the disused railway that served Leith Docks as it follows the Water of Leith inland through what was once its most industrial stretch, then cuts through some of the best parkland within the city. Leith, historically the port for Edinburgh, has a fascinating international history and many beautiful buildings. It is hard to imagine now, but this is where the game of golf took root in Scotland, Leith Links being the home of the game's senior club—not, as you might expect, the Royal and Ancient Club of St Andrews, but the Honourable Company of Edinburgh Golfers, who eventually moved from Leith to Muirfield.

Times have changed in Leith, with the passing of the rail link for one thing, but many cruise ships now visit on their way to the Orkneys, Shetlands, Faeroes or Iceland.

The Royal Yacht *Britannia* is now permanently berthed at Leith and is open to the public. This beautiful ship travelled over 1 million miles to every corner of the globe on 968 royal and official visits. Launched in 1953 at John Brown's Clyde shipyard, she continued an unbroken tradition of Royal yachts stretching back 300 years to the reign of Charles II. Now she has made the port of Leith her final home.

Like many an international seaport Leith once had a wicked reputation, but as the maritime industries have declined there is a sense of rejuvenation in the air. It still retains those foreign flavours, Dutch, French, Scandinavian and Italian, in its architecture. One of its newer buildings, the huge edifice of the Scottish Executive offices, dominates a large part of the former dock area. The front of this building is a fitting place to start this route.

Make your way to Commercial Street, then turn left into Sandport Street and join the Water of Leith Walkway. Head upstream to

INFORMATION

Distance: 12 km (7.5 miles). Circular route.

Start and finish: Commercial Wharf, Leith.

Map: OS Landranger 66 and Spokes Edinburgh Cycle Map.

Terrain: Cycle path and quiet city streets. Flat city route.

Refreshments: Cafe, restaurants and pubs in Leith and other places along the route.

The Royal Yacht *Britannia*

Scottish Executive –
Victoria Quay

where you will see a blue cycleway sign marking the fact that you have now joined National Cycle route 75. If you were to stay on this, it would lead you ultimately to Bell's Bridge in the heart of Glasgow. Keep to the north bank of the Water of Leith, which you will soon notice becomes the route of the old railway.

Before long you start to pass under the road bridges of North Leith and Chancelot, following the signs for Canonmills. It would be an interesting exercise to count the bridges you meet, as there are at least twenty-five. One of the grandest spans the path through Warriston cemetery, and the pillars at railway height are most impressive. They are also a good marker, because 150 m later you leave the track, on the right, immediately before a substantial bridge which crosses the Water of Leith, to drop down via the sports field into Warriston Crescent, a fine row of houses. A plaque on number 10 commemorates the fact that Frederic Chopin, Polish composer, stayed here in October 1848.

Inverleith Row, the main road at the end of Warriston Crescent, is the busiest road you will encounter. If there are younger or less experienced riders in your party, use the Pelican crossing to cross the road, then ride the short distance north to Inverleith Terrace Lane where you turn left and soon join Rocheid Path.

This is Canonmills, at one time the centre of the Edinburgh milling industry. The valley of the Water of Leith, then called the 'Dean', had many mills, most of them for the grinding of grain. There were also some 'waulk' mills for the fulling, that is, the cleansing and thickening of cloth. These became valuable sources of revenue to their proprietors and the City of Edinburgh. A charter from King Robert in 1329 consigned to Edinburgh the port of Leith with its mills, but these were not further specified. However, in 1423 a retired abbot of Holyrood House feued the 'Canoune Millis', part of his pension, to the burgh of Edinburgh for five years, this old connection being preserved in the place-name Canonmills.

Turn right into Arboretum Avenue, the main access to the Royal Botanic Gardens, arguably the finest in the world. They have always had a great connection with Leith, no doubt many of the early specimens arriving via the

Colourful cargo

docks. In 1661, Sir Robert Sibbald, one of the founders of the Royal College of Physicians of Edinburgh and the University's first Professor of Medicine, started what was then called the Physic Garden near Holyrood, growing medicinal herbs. It then moved to a site now occupied by Waverley Station; in 1766 it was relocated to Leith Walk, and then was established at its present site in the 1820s. It now extends to over eighty acres, and is well worth a visit at any time of year.

Turn left at the cycleway sign opposite the main gate into Inverleith Park, and follow the main path along a splendid tree-lined avenue, to East Fettes Avenue. Cross with care into Carrington Road and past the imposing Fettes College. Craigleith Hill Avenue then takes you all the way to Groathill Avenue, where you turn left down to the tennis courts, seventy metres away, and right onto a railway path again.

This cycleway will take you all the way back to Leith if you bear right after crossing Ferry Road. Carry straight on at the next junction, Five Ways junction, then after 200 metres turn right before entering Victoria Park. At the other side of the park the cycleway continues to Steadfastgate and familiar territory. From here turn left and retrace the first part of the route back to Leith. Bear other path users in mind as you ride towards the docks, as the path is well surfaced, gently downhill most of the way and it is easy to generate a good pace. Of course there is the lure of gastronomic delights at the far end.

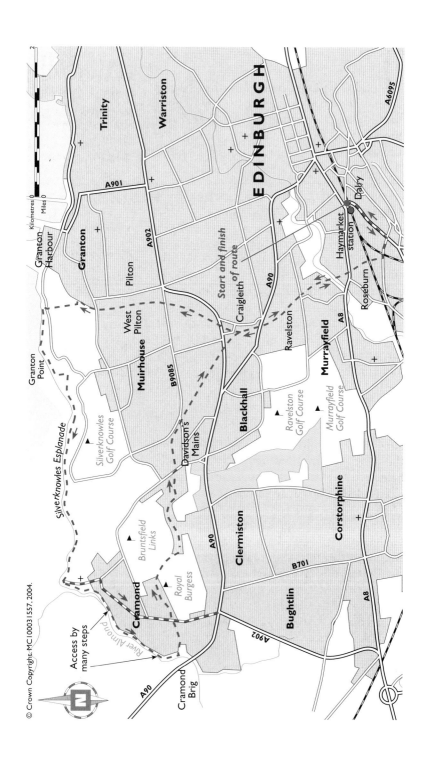

© Crown Copyright MC100031557, 2004.

Kilometres 0
Miles 0

Granton Harbour
Granton Point
Silverknowles Esplanade
Access by many steps
River Almond
Cramond Brig
A90

Cramond
Royal Burgess
Bruntsfield Links
Silverknowles Golf Course
Davidson's Mains
B9085
Muirhouse
West Pilton
Pilton
Granton
A901
A902
Trinity
Warriston

EDINBURGH

Start and finish
Craigleith of route

Blackhall
Ravelston
Ravelston Golf Course
A90
Clermiston
B701
A902
Bughtlin
A8

Corstorphine
Murrayfield Golf Course
Murrayfield
A8

Roseburn
Haymarket station
Dalry
A6095

HAYMARKET TO CRAMOND

This route, which is 77% totally traffic free, will take you from the west end of Edinburgh city centre to the coast at Cramond and back. Using mainly old railways for the off-road sections, the ride is surprisingly direct, as will be particularly apparent to car drivers who are used to the stop-start routine of the rush hour.

From Haymarket Station join Dalry Road where cyclists can use the Greenway bus lanes. Carry on along here for 700 m to the junction with Murieston Crescent. Here an on-street cycle route is clearly signposted to where the railway cycle track begins at Russell Road close to Murrayfield Stadium. This route follows the line of the Granton, Leith and Barnton branch railway, which was opened by the Caledonian Railway Company in 1861. This originally carried coal and other freight to Granton harbour, but later passenger services were started with branches to Leith and Barnton. The railway was closed in stages between 1951 and 1986.

After passing Coltbridge railway viaduct and the steps down to the Water of Leith Walkway below, the cycleway passes under Upper Coltbridge Terrace where the Gallery of Modern Art is located. Almost 2 km further on, the cycleway passes the platform of Craigleith Station and goes under Craigleith Road. Just past this, to the east of the path, is a supermarket. This was built on the site of Craigleith Quarry, which supplied the stone for the Usher Hall, most of the grand houses of the New Town, and even Buckingham Palace in London. This is also the spot where the Barnton branch line leaves the main route and goes off in a westerly direction, and this route will be used for the return journey.

INFORMATION

Distance: 20 km (12.5 miles). Circular route.

Start and finish: Haymarket Railway Station.

Map: OS Landranger 66 and Spokes Edinburgh Cycle Map.

Terrain: Cycle path, suburban roads, riverside walkway and foreshore promenade. Flat route generally but two steep sets of stairs to be negotiated on the riverside walkway at Cramond. An alternative route has been described.

Refreshments: A variety of facilities in the west end of the city near the start, pub grub and bistro at Cramond.

Ancient tree on the banks of the Almond

Cramond Kirk – the most ancient of churches

Continue on another 700 m or so to the bridge over Ferry Road, where the cycleway bisects once again. Take the route to the left. This route was originally constructed by Spokes. It finishes just north of West Granton Road where it joins Caroline Park Avenue.

When West Shore Road is reached, turn right and continue along it for 150 m, then turn left. Within 100 m, a wide tarmac path once more appears heading in the direction of the shore. This is the beginning of the Esplanade which will take you the remaining 5 km to Cramond. On a clear day many of the islands in the Firth of Forth can be seen, including Inchmickery, Inchcolm and, of course, the closest of all, Cramond Island.

Halfway between Granton and Cramond a large house is visible at the top of the escarpment. This is Craigcrook Castle, which was built as a keep in 1545 for the defence and provision of Edinburgh in the event of a siege.

On now to the ancient village of Cramond. Its name was originally spelt Caer Almond, and meant simply 'the fort on the mouth of the river Almond'. Just before the promenade turns along the riverside, a large tower-house can be seen off to the left. This is Cramond Tower. Not much is known about its origins, but it was renovated recently and is now used as a private residence. In AD 142 engineers of the Roman army chose this spot to build a harbour and fort to service the construction of Antonine's Wall. Excavated by archaeologists in 1954, the fort, made of clay and stone, was very large. It had towers at each corner, four gates and 20-foot-high walls which were 27 feet thick. A model and the major finds of the excavation are kept in the Huntly House Museum in the Canongate, and a plan of part of the structure can be seen on the site of the fort next to Cramond Kirk.

Old Cramond Bridge

A village grew up around the fort's east rampart. The people grew oats and barley and herded pigs which they traded with the Roman soldiers. Although the Roman presence in this area only lasted a few decades, it had a profound effect on the Gododdin. Long after the Romans had left the area, the tribespeople continued to live in the fort, making repairs and even carrying out new building work in the Roman style. They seem to have embraced the Christian religion, for they used the basilica within the Principia of the fort as a place of worship. Cramond Kirk stands on the spot today.

Around AD 600, the Gododdin King, Mynyddog, moved his tribe's headquarters to Din Eidyn (Dun Edin), which is Edinburgh Castle Rock. With the Romans gone, the Gododdin were being threatened by a new enemy from the south in the form of the

Pushing on up the river Almond

Roseburn Bridge

Angles of Northumbria, who by the middle of the seventh century had defeated the Gododdin and taken control of the area around Midlothian.

Cramond village and its little church survived. In Victorian times it became popular as the summer home of Edinburgh's well-to-do residents. In 1860 Queen Victoria visited Cramond, staying at Cramond House. Today this delightful village has lost none of its character and is a pleasant spot for a breath of sea air.

There are two ways to return to Edinburgh. The first is to continue along the path through the deep gorge of the River Almond. It was here that the iron-milling industry grew up, and in the early part of the 1700s four mills worked side by side between the village and Old Cramond Brig. The ruins of Fairafar Mill can still be seen today. From Cramond this path is 1.5 km and ends at Brae Park, a short distance from Old Cramond Brig. Look out for a great variety of wild life on the river which includes kingfishers and otters. The only slight problem with this route is the connection of the middle third of the path which is via two sets of steps, over 60 in each, where bikes will have to be carried.

At the end of the path turn left on to Brae Park and continue to the junction with Whitehouse Road. Cross this road with the aid of the Toucan Crossing and head along Barnton Avenue West. At this point the two alternative routes have once again come together.

Steps up to Cramond village

The second route simply uses a series of streets to get from the end of the esplanade at Cramond to the same point at Barnton Avenue West. This is as follows: at the end of the esplanade turn left into Cramond Glebe Road and commence uphill to the junction with Whitehouse Road. Here turn right along Whitehouse Road for a kilometre to the junction of Barnton Avenue West where the two alternatives once again merge.

At the end of Barnton Avenue West follow the cycle path between two golf courses to Barnton Avenue and continue to the end of this, as it

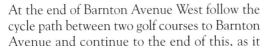

Swan contemplates the weir on the River Almond

twists and turns, to Cramond Road South. Cross this road by the Toucan Crossing and carry on into Silverknowes Terrace which soon becomes Silverknowes Drive before it ends at Silverknowes Road. Cross this and join Silverknowes Road East where almost immediately the railway path appears on the right side of the road. Carry on along this path for over a kilometre to the junction at Craigleith, where this path merges with the path taken on the outer leg of the ride. From here retrace the route back to the start.

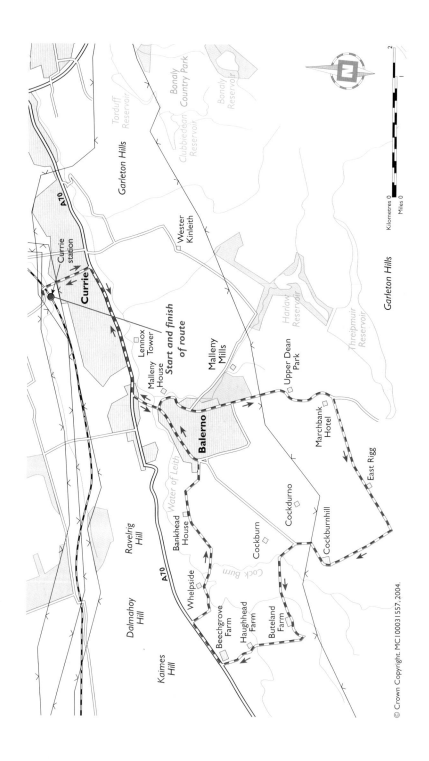

Garleton Hills

Torduff Reservoir

Bonaly Country Park

Clubbiedean Reservoir

Bonaly Reservoir

A70

Currie station

Currie

Lennox Tower

Malleny Tower House

Start and finish of route

Wester Kinleith

Malleny Mills

Harlaw Reservoir

Threipmuir Reservoir

Garleton Hills

Balerno

Upper Dean Park

Marchbank Hotel

East Rigg

Water of Leith

Bankhead House

Cockburn

Cockdurno

Cockburnhill

Ravelrig Hill

A70

Whelpside

Cock Burn

Dalmahoy Hill

Kaimes Hill

Beechgrove Farm

Haughhead Farm

Buteland Farm

Kilometres 0   2
Miles 0   1

THE BALERNO LOOP

Balerno was the end of the Caledonian Railway branch line along the Water of Leith, and an ideal launching pad for the many walkers bent on a day in the Pentland Hills in the first half of the twentieth century. It is thought that Winston Churchill may have been the last passenger to board a train from Balerno, his official train having used the line on a visit to Edinburgh. Therefore it is very fitting that this route should start from a railway station.

Leave the station and turn right on to Curryhill Road and carry on to the T-junction with Lanark Road West. Here turn left, whilst at all times taking care on this often busy road. Turn right at the next junction, Kirkgate, and carry on downhill and over the bridge which spans the Water of Leith. At the other side take the access path on to the Water of Leith Walkway, which is also part of Sustrans National Cycle Route 75 linking Edinburgh and Glasgow. Proceed west along this off-road cycle route to its end at Bridge Road, Balerno, and turn left and cross the Water of Leith once again before turning left on to Bavelaw Road which links to Mansfield Road.

The name of the village itself has a distinct foreign flavour—is it Italian or even Irish? There has been no conclusive explanation, but where else could you ride from suburban comfort to really wild moor and mountain in twenty minutes? The contrast is even greater when you consider a fit cyclist can ride from Princes Street to this part of the Pentlands in less than an hour. Is any other major city in the world so well situated?

There was a large paper mill at Balerno. Sadly only the office entrance still stands. The smell

INFORMATION

Distance: 20 km (12.5 miles). Circular route.

Start and finish: Currie Railway Station.

Map: OS Landranger 65, Edinburgh and West Lothian Cycle Maps.

Terrain: Cycle path and minor roads. Middle section is very hilly.

Refreshments: Places in Currie and Balerno.

Currie

National signing and
Currie Kirk

of the Spanish esparto grass, the principal raw material in making of its fine papers, is long gone. Even after the railway closed, the mill worked on and there were always two or three lorries stacked high with the large bales of grass parked in the village, waiting to deliver their load and return to Granton, which at that time was the chief British port for the importation of this crop.

Once on Mansfield Road you are headed for the hills—though there is a brief respite at Malleny Millgate. You then enter a region of hedgeless open fields, but the route still climbs, particularly steeply at Upper Dean Park.

When you reach the top of the hill do not go straight on towards the wildlife reserve, but turn right at Red Moss and ride along its northern fringes. Ian Finlay, in his splendid book *The Lothians*, claims that 'the dark vistas of heather and black peat hags might easily be in the midst of Lewis or Sutherland'. These are the moors where the Water of Leith has its source some five or six kilometres to the west. Caught in fading light the scene does not seem to belong here, a piece of the Highlands found in the wrong place, but beautiful just the same.

Ride the long straight road with mature trees on the right and the moss on the left, the Pentlands dominating the vista across the fields and the noise of wild fowl on the western end of the Threipmuir Reservoir always with you. The trees look like an avenue which becomes more dense at the western end. The roadside ditch, running with clean water, is no doubt a haven for frogs and newts.

At the end of the road turn your back on the Pentlands and head north on another beech-lined avenue. There is a tremendous swoop down past Cockburnhill farm, then you turn left into Cockburn Hill Road. It is strange to see a street sign in the midst of the country. Follow the uphill undulations through Buteland Farm to the triangle with the warning of a ford ahead. After turning right you will see the white bridge at the ford, which is dry, but watch out for mossy deposits never-theless. Dark vistas of heather

Water of Leith

lie off to your left and the watershed is so indeterminate that an old minister at Dolphinton once claimed that it was possible for a salmon to come up from the Tweed by this route and go down into the Clyde!

When you reach the A70, the infamous 'Lang Whang', turn right opposite the old American airfield, then take the first turning on the right to Whelpside. The Lang Whang was an old coaching route. The fantastic old names live on! Little Vantage is a farm you pass, then there's Boll o' Bere, and a little further away an inn called Jenny's Toll. It was at this inn that two resurrection men (body-snatchers) took rest and refreshment while the bodies they had stolen from Lanark kirkyard, for dissection by the anatomists in Edinburgh, waited under a load of peats and straw on the cart outside. However, the corpses were rescued and re-interred by a posse from Currie. It is not recorded what happened to the body snatchers.

Some of the farm buildings at Glenbrook have undergone stylish refurbishment—a definite sign that you are returning to civilisation. The road delivers you to the outskirts of Balerno, and all that is required is to turn left on to Johnsburn Road, at the end of which Bridge Road takes you back to the cycle route to retrace your way back to Currie Station.

Much of this ride lies above the 200 metre contour and can be exposed, even in summer. Be prepared. Do not be afraid to turn back.

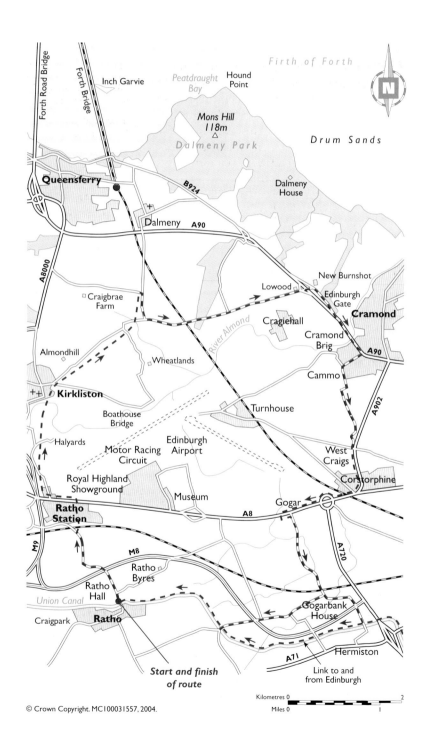

Firth of Forth

Forth Road Bridge

Forth Bridge

Inch Garvie

Peatdraught Bay

Hound Point

Mons Hill 118m

Dalmeny Park

Drum Sands

Queensferry

Dalmeny

B924

A90

Dalmeny House

A8000

Craigbrae Farm

New Burnshot

Lowood

Edinburgh Gate

Cragiehall

Cramond

Cramond Brig

A90

River Almond

Almondhill

Wheatlands

Cammo

A902

Kirkliston

Boathouse Bridge

Turnhouse

Halyards

Motor Racing Circuit

Edinburgh Airport

West Craigs

Royal Highland Showground

Museum

Corstorphine

Ratho Station

A8

Gogar

M9

M8

Ratho Byres

A720

Ratho Hall

Union Canal

Gogarbank House

Craigpark

Ratho

Hermiston

A71

Link to and from Edinburgh

Start and finish of route

Kilometres 0 2

Miles 0 1

© Crown Copyright. MC100031557, 2004.

WESTERN FRINGES: AIRPORT PERIMETERS

This route started out as a challenge to circumnavigate Edinburgh Airport by the shortest route, which in reality was never going to be that short. However, the many cycle facilities in this area helped to define the chosen route, and finally the lure of the Union Canal extended it even further.

The route begins at the Bridge Inn at Ratho, whether you choose to come by bicycle from the centre of Edinburgh along the towpath of the Union Canal or by car. Head north and follow the road towards Ratho Station. (However, these days there is no station.)

The Forth Bridge comes into sight as you reach the crest of the rise, but do not get carried away on the descent, for you want to turn right onto the cycle path before the railway, signposted to Ratho Station. The footbridge you use to cross the busy A8 road can be seen as you cross the railway. All that is required is a steady run along Station Road to the footbridge.

INFORMATION

Distance: 22 km (13.8 miles). Circular route.

Start and finish: Ratho Bridge.

Map: OS Landranger 65, Edinburgh and West Lothian Cycle Maps.

Terrain: Road, roadside cycle lanes, off-road cycle track, canal towpath. Route is generally flat.

Refreshments: Bridge Inn, Ratho, and the Cramond Brig Hotel.

Boats moored at Ratho

Oh Mum!

If you are lucky you might see aerial action from the elevated viewpoint of the footbridge, as it is close to the airport runway. Then follow the cycle route signs for Kirkliston, passing one of the busiest roundabouts in Scotland. It might well come as a surprise to find that a railway once came right through this spot, and even more surprising to find rabbits playing near this busy interchange.

Within metres the noise of the traffic fades, the old railway is lined with broom, hawthorn and elder, and you find yourself in the countryside. The track runs straight as an arrow to Kirkliston.

Entry to Kirkliston is over the fine bridge across the River Almond. Ride on into Auldgate, still on the line of the railway, and continue towards Dalmeny. The roar of an outbound airliner might be heard and a Search and Rescue Sea King helicopter might be seen low overhead bound for the Army Head-quarters (Scotland), 3 km to the east.

The final few hundred metres of railway path is lined with Scots pines, quite unusual track-side trees, but providing an impressive avenue. There are fine views across the fields as you pass between the trees, particularly to the elegant towers of Carlowrie to the east. Drop down off the railway to the right, 300 m after the pines finish, on to the road, then head east past the Army Headquarters and through the cutting at Craigiehill Quarry to the A90 near Edinburgh Gate. Initially you use the old road,which takes you across the A90, then continue on the cycle track alongside the dual carriageway to Cramond Bridge.

The Bridge Inn, Ratho

It is worth pausing to see the old Cramond Brig Toll, or even diverting down to the old bridge, before continuing along the pavement towards the city. After 50 m cross the A90 using the Pelican Crossing, turn left and continue to Cammo Road, then skirt the Cammo estate passing the impressive tower-shaped folly en route to Maybury.

Use the path all the way to the bypass interchange, where it becomes wider and well signed. Ride all the way west to Gogar where you will find a bridge across the A8. Take this to Gogar Station Road where you now pass the world headquarters of the Royal Bank of Scotland. Then turn right at Gogarbank and carry on to Gogar Moor Bridge, where the Union Canal towpath is joined.

Once more you are plunged into countryside and the relaxing ride along to Ratho is the final contrast of this multi-faceted tour.

That is unless, as I said at the beginning of the chapter, you have chosen to ride out from Edinburgh. If so, then once you have joined the canal towpath you would of course head east, back from whence you came.

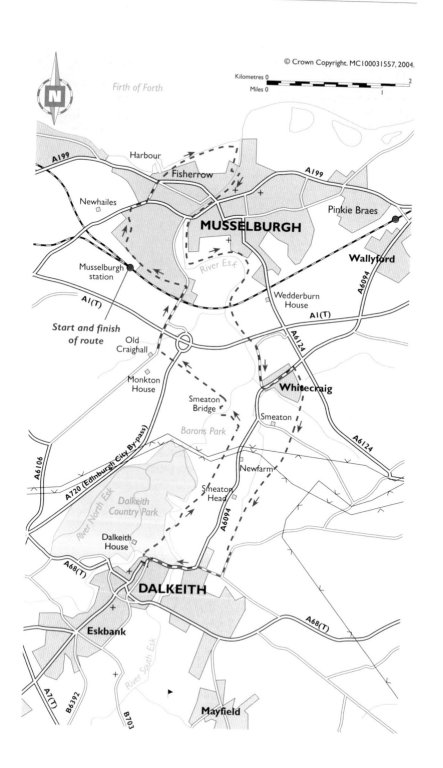

© Crown Copyright. MC100031557, 2004.

MUSSELBURGH TO DALKEITH

Musselburgh has been a port of some importance from the time of the Romans, who built the first harbour where Fisherrow Harbour now stands, a fort at Inveresk and the first bridge over the Esk. It is thought that, close to the fort, was some kind of temple to Apollo. Inveresk retained its religious significance in Christian times. There was a church there in the eleventh century known as Muscilburg, and lands in the area were gifted to the monks of Dunfermline Abbey, who held them until the Reformation.

Musselburgh is known as the Honest Toon. The burghers of the town protected the Regent of Scotland, Thomas Randolph, when he was threatened by an English army just after Robert the Bruce's death. When they were offered a reward for their devotion by the Earl of Mar, they declined, saying that they had only been doing their duty to the Regent. Mar then replied: 'Sure you are a set of honest fellows.' From that time the town has proudly borne the motto *Honestas*.

The area around Musselburgh has been the scene of some famous battles, starting with the

INFORMATION

Distance: 20 km (12.5 miles). Circular route.

Start and finish: Musselburgh Station, or Fisherrow Harbour where there is car parking.

Map: OS Landranger 66 and Spokes Midlothian Cycle Map.

Terrain: Suburban streets, cycle path, estate road and river-side path. Route is generally flat.

Refreshments: Full facilities in Musselburgh and Dalkeith.

Dalkeith House

Battle of Pinkie in September 1547. This was a terrible defeat for the Scots, inflicted by Henry VIII's army during the 'Rough Wooing'. The second was the Battle of Carberry in June 1567. This is a most interesting battle in that not a shot was fired nor any blow struck. At this confrontation Mary Queen of Scots was urged by the Confederate Lords to rid herself of Bothwell, her third husband. She eventually agreed: Bothwell was given safe conduct to leave the country and spent the rest of his life in exile.

Many of the town's buildings are in the Georgian style but some pre-date that period. Two of note are the Tolbooth, built in 1496, and sixteenth-century Pinkie House. The latter is now part of the famous Loretto School.

The route starts at Musselburgh Station. Head out of the station in a northern direction and within a few metres a roundabout is reached. Here turn left on to Clayknowes Crescent and follow it as it snakes through the housing estate of the same name, to end at Newhailes Road. Turn right on to this busy road and within 300m a roundabout is reached. Keeping vigilant, carry straight on to the signalled junction with North High Street and then turn left into Harbour Road. At the end of this is Fisherrow Harbour. (The stretch between the end of Clayknowes Road and Harbour Road is very short. If you are not confident cycling on this busy road it will not take long to walk.)

Fisherrow harbour

The Old Bridge,
Musselburgh

From Fisherrow Harbour, follow the promenade, passing Loretto Playing Fields, to the River Esk, where it crosses the river by Goose Green Footbridge. Here, turn right into Esk Side East and follow the river, passing under the Bridge at Bridge Street, and continue along the eastern bank to the old bridge. This medieval bridge stands on the same site as that built by the Romans. From here the route crosses Mall Avenue into Station Road, to where the river Esk Walkway starts following the river bank.

Follow the walkway for a little less than 1.5 km past the site of a Roman fort and Monkton Hall Golf Course, situated on the other side of the river, to where there is a footbridge across which the cycleway to Edinburgh is routed. From here you are now on National Cycle Route 1 on its way south. Continue along this route for 2 km, ending at the point where it passes under the bridge carrying the A1 above. Then follow Cowpits Road north to the A6094 at Whitecraig.

Turn left and follow the A6094 for the short distance to the end of the village past the Dolphin Inn and there on the other side of the road the cycle route is signposted for Ormiston 5 miles.

This is our table,
you can't sit here

After a little under 1 km at Smeaton, the route comes to a double-arched railway bridge. Carry on through the right hand arch, keeping to the west path, and within 2 km the path reaches the B6414 Elphinstone Road at the Thornybank Industrial Estate at the edge of Dalkeith.

Here turn right and continue to follow Route 1 signs to the roundabout and carry straight on to Musselburgh Road, where, after a short distance, it turns at right angles, only to do so again in the opposite direction within a few metres. At the T-junction turn right and follow this road through the gates into Dalkeith Country Park, where on the left Dalkeith House is located.

The De Graham family built the original Castle in the twelfth century, making it one of the oldest residences in Midlothian. It passed into the hands of the house of Douglas, but after 300 years was then bought by the Scott family, one of whom married Charles II's son, the Duke of Monmouth. At their marriage the couple became the Duke and Duchess of Monmouth, Duke and Duchess of Buccleuch and Count and Countess of Dalkeith, and the castle at Dalkeith became the Palace of Dalkeith.

In the summer months the grounds, now a country park, are open to the public. It contains a deer forest, thought to be the only remnant of the ancient Caledonian Forest still in existence in southern Scotland, and many other interesting features. There is a charge to enter and visit the park's attractions, so if you are going to use its facilities please pay at the gate. The park management permits cyclists to go through the park at no charge, if they are using it for access purposes only, but you must follow the main access road through the park. However, this route may be subject to change. Do not deviate on to smaller paths, tracks or other areas. There are many horses on the estate. Please treat them with respect at all times. If they are passing, stop and do not make loud noises around them. If these simple rules are

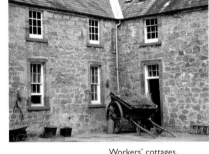

Workers' cottages, Dalkeith estate

observed no one will have any problems about you being there. In the winter, when the park is officially closed, the gates are left open to allow reasonable access, but of course the same rules apply.

Carry on through the park in a northerly direction, crossing the River North Esk on two occasions, firstly at Laundry Bridge and then again at Smeaton Bridge. Continue under the A720 to the edge of the park at Old Craighall on the B6415. Here turn right on to Craighall Road, which has signs with the letters RR, indicating cyclists' Ring Route. Follow this route north to the second roundabout where the National Cycle Route Signs are displayed once again, but this time they are guiding the cyclist west to Edinburgh. Turn left into a small housing estate following the cycle sign for Musselburgh Station. There is a plethora of National Route signs in this area, as the route twists and turns, first through this estate, then on to a children's play area. Another tip here is to follow the line of the electricity pylons overhead. Go through the play area, and then cross a road and on to a footpath. At the end of this, proceed along Muckets Avenue to Whitehill Farm Road. Here turn left and within a few metres the roundabout at the start of the route is reached. Turn left here and cross the bridge back to the station.

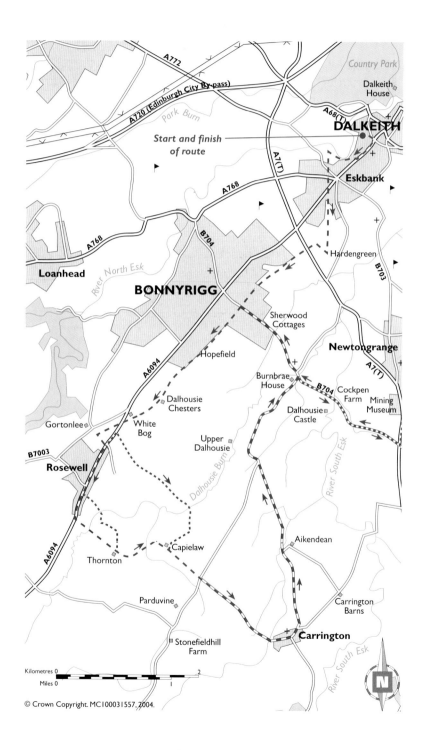

Country Park

A772

A720 (Edinburgh City By-pass)

Park Burn

Dalkeith House

A68(T)

DALKEITH

Start and finish of route

A7(T)

Eskbank

A768

Hardengreen

B704

B703

A768

Loanhead

River North Esk

BONNYRIGG

Sherwood Cottages

Newtongrange

A6094

Hopefield

Burnbrae House

A7(T)

Cockpen Farm

B704

Mining Museum

Dalhousie Chesters

Dalhousie Castle

Gortonlee

White Bog

Upper Dalhousie

River South Esk

B7003

Dalhousie Burn

Rosewell

A6094

Aikendean

Capielaw

Thornton

Carrington Barns

Parduvine

Carrington

Stonefieldhill Farm

River South Esk

Kilometres 0 — 2
Miles 0 — 1

N

© Crown Copyright. MC100031557, 2004.

DALKEITH TO ROSEWELL AND CARRINGTON

Dalkeith has a long and eventful history starting in feudal times. It was first mentioned in a charter of David I gifting 52 acres of land to the monks of Holyrood Abbey in 1128. As mentioned in the Musselburgh chapter, Dalkeith Castle was built by the De Grahams in the twelfth century.

Among places of interest in and around Dalkeith is Maiden Bridge, to be found in Waterfall Park. This bridge got its name because Princess Margaret, eldest daughter of Henry VII of England, who was betrothed to King James IV of Scotland, passed across it on her way to be married at Newbattle Abbey. This eventually led to James IV becoming heir to the English throne after the death of Queen Elizabeth I, and to the Union of the Crowns.

Newbattle Abbey is 500 m south of Maiden Bridge. The Cistercian monks first came to this area in 1140 from Melrose, the 'aldbotyl' or old house, to Newbattle, the 'newbotyl' or new house. This district is now known once again by its ancient name of Monklands. It was the monks who began coalmining in Midlothian, and until recently most of the collieries were in areas which the Newbattle monks had first mined. Sadly, the industry in Midlothian has now all but died out.

Newbattle Abbey was burned down twice, once by Richard II in 1387 and the second time by the Earl of Hertford in 1544. After the second fire it was not rebuilt, but much of the stone went to build Newbattle House on the same site, which incorporates some remains of the abbey, including the crypt and a chapel.

INFORMATION

Distance: 21 km (13miles). Circular route.

Start and finish: Car park on Old Edinburgh Road, Dalkeith.

Map: OS Landranger 66 and Spokes Midlothian Cycle Map.

Terrain: Railway path of various surfaces. Asphalt to compacted mud. First half is flat followed by undulating stretches with some short steep hills.

Refreshments: Places in Rosewell.

Carrington Kirk (now a graphic studio)

Cycle route at Dalkeith

The house was taken over by the Army during the Second World War and later became an adult education college. This closed in the 1980s, and the house operates today as a Conference Centre.

I recommend that you cycle around these interesting sites, either before you start this route or on your return—if you still have the energy.

The route begins at the car park just off Old Edinburgh Road. Turn right out of the car park and head for the junction with Eskbank Road and turn right. This road is part of National Cycle Route 1. Carry on past St David's Church, then take the first right into Cemetery Road. Here immediately on the left the footpath/cycleway along the banks of the River North Esk begins. Follow this path, almost to Glen Esk Viaduct, to where the cycleway to Penicuik goes off to the left and doubles back in a southerly direction.

Glen Esk viaduct, constructed in 1847 by the North British Railway Company, was restored in 1992 by Edinburgh Greenbelt Trust.

Take the path in the southerly direction and follow it continuously to where it comes to a T-junction with a rough path. Here turn right and follow this path to where it joins the bridge which takes cyclists and pedestrians over the busy A7 trunk road. At the other side the formal cycle route begins again, using the solum of the Edinburgh to Peebles Railway which was closed in 1969, all the way through Bonnyrigg, Lasswade and Roslin to Penicuik.

Within 1.5 km of the recommencement of the cycle route the traveller passes through the south part of Bonnyrigg and Lasswade, which today are physically joined together.

Making hay while the sun shines

Collectively, then, this is a comparatively modern place which grew from the area's industrial base of coalmining and paper-milling, although Lasswade's origins go back much further. The route continues for another 3 km to Rosewell, another small mining village with its uniform rows of miners' cottages.

Just before you enter the village turn left and join the minor road which soon joins the road through the centre of the village (To help you to recognise the point where you have to turn south from the cycleway, look out for Rosewell's fine brick church on the other side of the adjacent field). When you reach this point you have three choices. If you are looking for a bit of adventure and you are riding a mountain bike then take the first route given below. This route is recommended only for experienced cyclists—though they do not have to be mountain bikers. The other two routes are much easier, but all three have stretches of unmade track to negotiate, and all end up at the same point.

Route 1: Turn left away from Rosewell and carry on for some 300 m to where there is a narrow minor road on the right. Take this road, and within a short distance it becomes an unmade track. There are some very rutted and uneven stretches and some very steep hills both to ascend and descend. This track runs for 2 km before it joins a better road at

Old water tower in Dalkeith (now an interesting dwelling)

Capielaw. This route should be given the respect it deserves. But that said, it's great fun.

Route 2 is easier but not the easiest! This time turn right and proceed through Rosewell. Turn left into Whitehill Road at the Rosewell Institute. As you continue down this road once again it becomes an unmade track, but this time not so rutted. This track turns and continues by the side of a high wall and then soon after reaches a junction. Turn right here and follow the road uphill. Turn left at the T-junction and continue for a short distance before turning left again. From here it is about 500 m to arrive at the same spot at Capielaw where Route 1 joins.

Route 3 is the easiest route of all. It starts as Route 2, but continues to the next road on the left with the bus turning area on the other side of the road. There is no name on this street, but there is a blue sign which says 'Whitehill Estate—Thornton Farm'. Here turn left and continue to the farm, where yet again the road reverts to a track. However, within a short distance the road becomes tarmac once again. You will soon come to the road junction described in Route 2 and thereafter, as with Route 2, continue for a short distance before turning left again. From here it is about 500 m to arrive at the same spot at Capielaw where Route 1 joins.

When all routes have merged at Capielaw continue south east to a fourway junction and carry straight on. From here it is 2 km to the beautiful little village of Carrington with its little church, now a graphic art studio. Look

Panorama of Scottish Mining Museum

out also for the ruins of the thirteenth century church of St Kentigern at the end of the village.

From here you join National Cycle Route 1 again—just follow the road in the direction of Cockpen and Dalkeith. After 4 km you join the B704 and head north in the direction of Bonnyrigg and Lasswade for just over a kilometre. At this point you will see a sign to rejoin the cycleway you were on at the beginning of your journey. Turn right into Waverley Court, at the end of which the cycleway begins. Once back on this cycleway you are soon riding over the A7 once again and retracing the route back to Dalkeith.

River South Esk, Dalkeith

One small detour from the route above! When you reach the B704, head south to the junction of the A7, turn left and within 200 m you come to the Scottish Mining Museum on both sides of the road. This is well worth a visit. However, I would advise you to return by the B704 as described above, since the A7 is not an easy road to cycle upon.

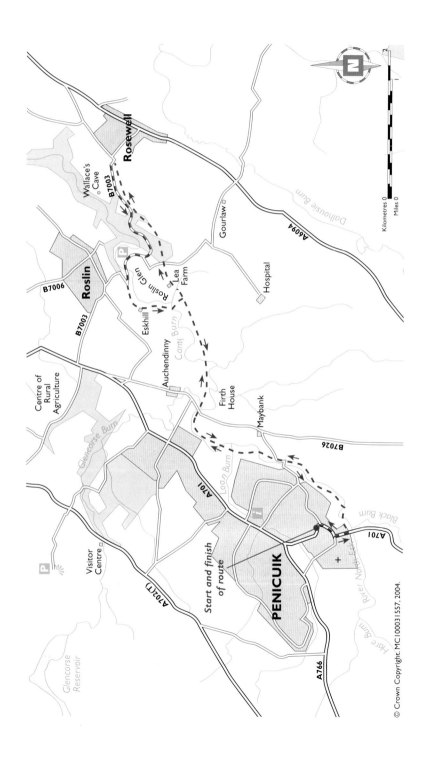

PENICUIK AND ROSLIN GLEN

Although Penicuik is dominated by the backdrop of the Pentland Hills to the west, this route follows the River North Esk north east through a heavily wooded valley, using the track bed of the old Edinburgh to Peebles Railway. Penicuik, whose name means the hill of the cuckoo, has existed for a long time as a tiny hamlet, but the town as it is today is comparatively new, being planned and laid out by Sir John Clerk in 1770. It has now grown to be a large dormitory town for those working in Edinburgh.

The main industry of the town, now all but disappeared, was papermaking. Valleyfield Mill, one of the earliest paper-mills, was used during the Napoleonic Wars to house French prisoners of war. 300 prisoners died whilst in captivity there, and local residents erected a monument to their memory which still stands today.

Leave the car park and join the High Street. Although cars can't make this manoeuvre, cyclists can. Carry on past the ruins of the ancient church of St Kentigern and the Town Hall to the corner of Bridge Street and turn left. Here on the West Street side stands an interesting building, now the Belgian Consulate and proudly flying the red, yellow and black flag of Belgium. Once on Bridge Street carry on for 150 m then turn left into Valleyfield Road. This takes you into a recently built housing estate. Take the third turning on the right at Bankmill View, and almost facing you is the entrance of the North Esk River Walk which joins the Penicuik to Dalkeith Cycleway.

This housing estate is built on the site of Valleyfield Mill mentioned earlier. To see the monument commemorating the French prisoners, carry on along Waterloo Bank on the opposite side of the road to Bankmill View, and there it stands on the edge of the estate. As the North Esk weaves its way down the glen, the

Ancient ruins of the church of St Kentigern

Penicuik

railway inevitably took a much straighter line, and so crosses the river several times. The first occasion is within 100 metres of the start. A newly landscaped park with a spring-fed pond, adopted by an ever-increasing colony of mallard, leads you to a splendid path alongside the river. Sluices and long-defunct mill lades are a major feature of this ride, as are many bridges and a couple of tunnels. The tarmac path gives way to a narrow stretch of single track between the river and a huge mill lade, but you soon rejoin the wide trackbed through Beeslack Woods. Wildlife is plentiful—look out for woodpeckers and grey squirrel.

A black bowstring bridge carries you into the first tunnel, long and incredibly dark even at midday. This emerges into the yard of Dalmore Paper Mill, the last surviving mill on the river; take care to ride between the fences marking the path alongside the factory yard. The second subway, the Firth Tunnel, leads you onto the splendid Firth Viaduct, offering a good view of the nearby Pentland Hills. This was designed by Thomas Bouch, architect of the ill-fated Tay Bridge, which collapsed one stormy night in 1879. However, there has been no trouble with this one! Look back and you will see the remains of the Old Woodhouselee Castle on a rocky outcrop.

Rosslyn Castle

The way continues along the cycle track past Rosslyn Castle station, with a sign made from seashells.

Here you may notice a difference in spelling from the village of Roslin. The double 's' is the older spelling, a combination of ross, meaning a rocky outcrop, and lin, a waterfall.

The cycleway ends at the junction with the A6094 and the B7003 near the village of Rosewell. Here turn left on to the B7003 which winds alongside the river once again. After a little over a kilometre the entrance to Roslin Glen Country Park is reached on the right. Here are many places of historic significance, including Rosslyn Collegiate Chapel which was built in 1446 by the Sinclairs, Earls of Orkney and Caithness. This is famous for its

Rosslyn Castle station

Apprentice Pillar and beautifully ornate carvings covering every surface. You can also see Rosslyn Castle, the main stronghold of the Sinclairs. During the Wars of Independence, an English army was heavily defeated by the Scots in 1303 near the castle. It played a key role in many conflicts over the years, and in 1650 was attacked by General Monk during Cromwell's invasion of Scotland. However the Sinclairs still own the castle, and part of it is habitable.

As the country park is so interesting it may be worthwhile making a detour to explore it and perhaps have a picnic by the river.

Once back on the B7003 the road crosses the river again, and 200 m further, at a hairpin bend at the bottom of a very steep hill, there is another entrance into the west part of Roslin Glen Country Park. Carry on straight through this beautiful woodland area, once the site of one of Scotland's largest gunpowder factories, and you come, once again, to the Penicuik to Dalkeith Cycleway, where you turn right and retrace the first quarter of the route back into the centre of Penicuik. The downside of doing this is that you will have to climb two sets of steps just prior to returning to the railway path. However, comfort yourself with the knowledge that these are a lot easier to negotiate than the steep hills offered by the on-road alternative.

The black bowstring bridge is followed by the first tunnel

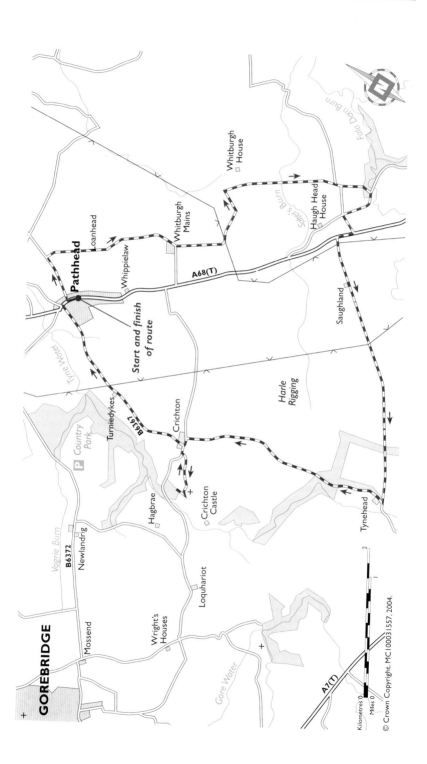

Whitburgh House

Haugh Head House

Folo Dam Burn

Whitburgh Mains

Solke's Burn

Loanhead

Whippielaw

Pathhead

A68(T)

Saughland

Start and finish of route

Tyne Water

Harle Rigging

Country Park

P

Turniedykes

B6367

Crichton

Crichton Castle

Tynehead

Hagbrae

Vogrie Burn

B6372

Newlandrig

Loquhariot

Mossend

Wright's Houses

Gore Water

GOREBRIDGE

A7(T)

Kilometres 0   1   2
Miles 0   1

© Crown Copyright. MC10003 I557, 2004.

THE PATHHEAD CIRCLE

The village of Pathhead lies on the eastern banks of the Tyne Water and is built along almost a kilometre stretch of the A68 trunk road. Pathhead was the site of a Roman marching camp on the Roman road known as Dere Street. The name 'Dere' is thought to come from the Anglo-Saxon kingdom of 'Deira'. The line of the Roman road would originally have been the 'road to Deira'. The A68 today follows this Roman road for a considerable distance.

The road out of Pathhead on the north side of the village is the B6367, signposted for Haddington. Carry on along this road for a short distance, some 600 m, to a right turn on to a minor road which is not signposted. Once on this road you soon begin to climb, passing some cottages at Loanhead and then continue up through pleasant woodland to Whitburgh Mains. Here take the left fork and continue past Whitburgh House, once the home of Sir Thomas Borthwick. Carry on along this road for 2 km to a T-junction. The day I cycled along this stretch I briefly disturbed a family of stoats, at least six, playing games on the road. Some disappeared into the undergrowth but two kept watch until I was safely past, no doubt to give the all-clear so that the game could continue. At the T-junction turn right. However, if you were to turn left, about 500 m along the road you would find the community of Fala Dam with its beautiful terraces of cottages, which are worth seeing. Once you return to the route the road soon comes to an end at the A68, where you must turn right on to this busy road. So take care! However, you are only on it for about 200 m before turning left on to the quiet B6458

INFORMATION

Distance: 17 km (10.6 miles). Circular route.

Start and finish: Pathhead Main Street, where car parking is plentiful.

Map: OS Landranger, sheet 66 and Spokes Midlothian Cycle Map.

Terrain: Minor roads. The first half of this route it undulating with stretches of steep ascent, one prolonged. The second half is less demanding.

Houses at Fala Dam

Crichton Kirk

signposted for Tynehead. This long straight road is bounded by moorland on both sides and rises gradually over almost 2 km before falling by the same distance to Tynehead.

At Tynehead turn right and follow the B6367 gradually downhill to the village of Crichton 3 km on. This stretch of road is tree-lined on one side with open moorland on the other. If you look over the moor you will catch a glimpse of Crichton Castle, a building of great historical importance.

This courtyard castle was built between the fourteenth and sixteenth centuries. The oldest part is the keep with its vaulted basement and pit prison. In the fifteenth century a new gatehouse of three storeys was added, then further buildings and ramparts finally enclosed the courtyard. Another block was added in the sixteenth century, in the Italian Renaissance style, with an arcaded, diamond-faced facade.

Outside the castle are the roofless stables, which are said to be haunted by the ghost of William Crichton.

The castle was a property of the Crichton family, and probably first built about 1370. In 1437, when James Stewart was only 6 years old, he was crowned king and became James II. Because the king was a child, Archibald, fifth Earl of Douglas, head of the grand and power-ful family of Black Douglases, was appointed Regent. When he died two years later, two men, Sir Alexander Livingstone and Sir William Crichton, schemed to take the place of the Douglases. In 1440 they invited the new Earl of Douglas, then only 16 years old, to dine with his brother and a friend at Edinburgh Castle. At the end of the meal the head of a black bull was brought to the table, and at this sign all three were murdered. This night of infamy is known as the 'Black Dinner'.

Crichton survived this heinous act unpunished and went on to found the nearby Collegiate Church, wherein priests were to pray for his salvation.

The entrance of the stable block

In 1488, during the reign of James IV, the Crichtons were charged with treason, and the property later passed to Patrick Hepburn, Lord Hailes, who was made Earl of Bothwell. One of the family was Patrick Hepburn, fourth Earl, and best known as the third husband of Mary, Queen of Scots. In 1559 the castle was besieged and captured by the Earl of Arran and, after the Earl of Bothwell escaped into exile, it was given to Francis Stewart, who added the Renaissance buildings. Francis Stewart was a brawler and a scoundrel, and as a consequence of his continued bad behaviour, in 1593 the castle was taken from him. Crichton Castle was passed on through many families before finally becoming the ruin that can be seen today.

Once in the little village of Crichton the castle is 1 km away and the way is well signposted. I recommend that you visit it, for it is one of the most interesting ruins in Scotland. On arriving at the cluster of large houses which lie at the end of the public road (look out for the one with the sun dial on its gable), you come to the Collegiate Church. This church, now the parish kirk, consisting of a choir and transept, is also fine place to visit, but you will have to do this on a Sunday.

Family of cyclists pedal through Crichton

Once you have returned to the village of Crichton, continue along the B6367 for 2.5 km following the signpost back to Pathhead.

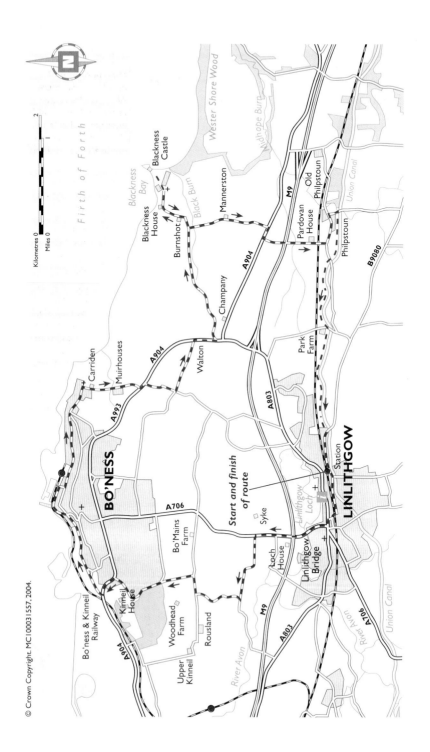

© Crown Copyright. MC100031557, 2004.

LINLITHGOW TO BO'NESS

Linlithgow first came to prominence during the reign of King David I (1124–53). He founded it as a Royal Burgh and built a manor house there with the church of St Michael next to it, roughly where the present palace stands. The palace, now in ruins, was built much later by a succession of Stewart kings.

After leaving Linlithgow Station, turn right on to Station Road and cycle up the first short hill which is typical of this fairly hilly route. Continue, past the Union Canal, into Strawberry Bank and head west on to Royal Terrace, which sweeps under the railway and joins Union Road. Turn right into St Johns Avenue and then left on to High Street. Take the first turning on the right into the A706, St Ninians Road. Carry on out of town and begin a steady but not arduous climb for 2 km, to the first junction past the B8029, and turn left on to a minor road. This road, with a sign stating that it is a 'No Through Road for Motor Vehicles', runs parallel to the main road for a short distance before turning west, meandering through fields as it goes.

Carry on along this road for 1.5 km to a T-junction, turn right and head north and uphill once again. At the top of the hill another T-junction is reached. This time turn right and carry on along this road for about 200 m, turn left and continue downhill towards the outskirts of Borrowstounness, or, to give it its more common name, Bo'ness. As this road turns through 90 degrees and on to Crawfield Road there is a rough path straight ahead which improves en route to its end at Kinneil House. Either take this path or turn left on to

Kinneil House

Doocot

Crawfield Road and head downhill towards Kinneil House, at which point this road changes its name to Provost Road.

Kinneil House, originally a twelfth-century keep, was the ancient seat of the Hamilton family. It was pillaged and burnt down in the sixteenth century when Protestants and Catholics fought for control of the country after the death of Mary Queen of Scots. The building which is visible today is an amalgam of the old keep and various later additions. It is in a remarkable state of preservation, having recently been re-roofed and re-floored.

Directly behind the house there are the remains of a workshop which was used by James Watt in the early development of the steam engine. Watt came to Kinneil in 1769, invited by Doctor John Roebuck to help develop an engine to deal with the problem of flooding in coal mines. However, these experiments were largely unsuccessful.

A few hundred metres to the west of Kinneil House is the site of the eleventh-century village of Kinneil. The ruins of the church gable are all that remains today. On leaving the grounds of Kinneil House, turn left into Provost Road and carry on to the junction with Snab Brae. Turn left here and head for a few metres to the roundabout with Grangemouth Road and then proceed along Kinneil Road to another roundabout. (If you want to avoid all these roundabouts, then halfway down Snab Brae, on the opposite side of the road, at the Clarence sign, there is a pedestrian access into Snab Lane. Follow this across Kinneil Road and at the end it joins the rough path which is Bo'ness foreshore path. Carry on to the east to where it joins Union Street only a few metres

Linlithgow Palace

from the entrance to the Bo'ness and Kinneil Railway.) Here turn left into Union Street and follow it around to the entrance of the Bo'ness and Kinneil Railway.

The Bo'ness and Kinneil Steam Railway was established in 1979. The Scottish Railway Preservation Society has transformed this site beside the old dock basin into the embodiment of a working steam railway. A Victorian station was brought lock, stock and barrel from Wormit in Fife, and rebuilt on this site. An engine shed dating from 1842 and a worker's cottage depicting life in the 1920s have also been preserved. Throughout the summer, SRPS run a regular service via Kinneil Halt to Birkhill Station—a distance of almost five miles.

From there it is but a short walk to the beautiful Avon Gorge where Birkhill Fire Clay Mine sits in the hillside. The mine contains 300-million-year-old fossils in the walls and roof. An audio-visual presentation shows exactly what it was like to work in a mine in the past.

Bo'ness Station

Blackness Castle

On leaving the railway, rejoin Union Street and turn left; then at the T-junction with Moss Road turn left. Follow this road through two name changes and a right-angle bend to where it becomes Carriden Brae. Keep going, climbing once again, to the junction with the A904. Here turn left then immediately right on to a minor road. After 500 m a crossroads is reached. Here turn left, and carry on to the junction with the A904 once again. Turn right and join this road for 300 m or so to the junction with the B903, follow this road for 3 km to Blackness and carry on through this little village to Blackness Castle, where the road ends on a promontory at the east end of Blackness Bay.

Blackness Castle stands on its rocky outcrop like a sentinel. There has probably been a harbour and some form of fortification here since Roman times. Some local historians have even said that this is the site of Ceir Eden, the end of the Antonine Wall. The present-day castle was built in stages between the fifteenth and sixteenth centuries by the Hamilton family. It has occasionally been used as a prison, and in fact at one time was Scotland's

chief state prison. Its unfortu-
nate inmates have included
Cardinal Beaton (1543), the
Earl of Angus (1544), and a
number of Covenantors held
there in 1660. From the time
of the Napoleonic Wars its
main use was as an artillery
fortress and an arsenal. It is
now being restored by Historic
Scotland.

Towpath, Union Canal

Follow the same road back out of Blackness,
but after a kilometre or so turn left on to the
B9109 and follow it to its end at the junction
with the A904. At this point the entrance to
the House of the Binns, the historic home of
the Dalyell Family, is a few metres to the right.
Today the house is the residence of Tam
Dalyell, the famous Westminster MP. His
ancestor and namesake General Tam Dalyell
raised the Royal Scots Greys here in 1681. The
house is run by the National Trust for Scotland
and is open to the public in the summer.

At the junction with the A904 turn right and
follow this busy road for 200 m, then turn left
on to the minor road signposted for Philpstoun.
Follow this road to its end at a T-junction, turn
left and after 200 m enter the small village of
Philpstoun. Look for a former church building
on the right at the T-junction and turn into a
small estate called Church Court. Turn right
and follow this road around to the left, and at
the end of it there is an access to the towpath
of the Union Canal. Carry on along the
towpath, heading west, for 4.5 km to where the
route began at Station Road, Linlithgow.

Cygnets – young swans

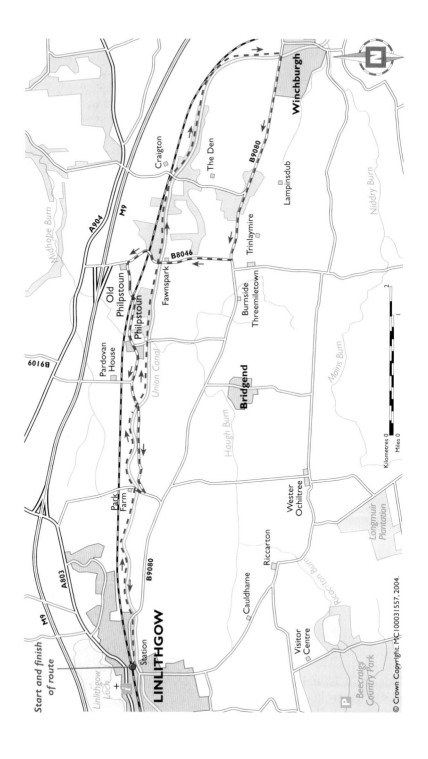

© Crown Copyright. MC100031557, 2004.

LINLITHGOW TO WINCHBURGH

This is the third chance to explore the wonders of Linlithgow before, this time, heading east along the Union Canal to Winchburgh.

After leaving Linlithgow Station, turn right on to Station Road and cycle up the first short hill, at the top of which you will find the Union Canal. On joining the towpath, turn left and head east.

After leaving Linlithgow the canal continues for 5 km to Philpstoun and then the same distance again to Winchburgh. This stretch of canal between Philpstoun and Niddry, just beyond Winchburgh, is in a cutting, sometimes as deep as 20 m, and represents a major feat of engineering, especially since it was constructed by hundreds of 'navvies' or navigators, with nothing more than pick and shovel.

The most notorious of these navvies were William Burke and William Hare who, having come over from Ireland, stayed on to start their infamous series of murders in Edinburgh.

The ride along the canal is very enjoyable. The wildlife is superb. The whole environment is full of interest and you are so close to everything and involved with it. A heron lifts from the reeds. There are coots galore, making a pretence at secrecy, and resident swans. The first I met was very friendly and crossed the canal to greet me, but the second, a cob, sitting right at the side of the towpath by the houses of Philpstoun, struck an aggressive posture, probably because his mate was sitting on eggs across the water.

From Winchburgh the canal snakes its way between several

INFORMATION

Distance: 15.7 km (9.74 miles).

Start and finish: Linlithgow Station.

Map: OS Landranger 65 and Spokes Midlothian Cycle Map.

Terrain: Mostly minor roads and canal towpath. This route is generally flat.

Refreshments: Tally Ho Hotel in Winchburgh.

Canal bridge at Winchburgh

Niddry Castle

bings, remnants of the shale oil industry's claim in this area, and passes Niddry Castle beyond the Edinburgh to Glasgow railwayline which runs parallel to the canal for most of the latter's length. You may want to extend your journey along the towpath for a further kilometre to take in this amazing piece of industrial history, before turning back to Winchburgh by the same route to continue on the main journey.

Until recently, Niddry Castle was a ruin, but in 1984 work was started to restore it as a habitable dwelling. The castle was built at the end of the fifteenth century by the Seton family, whose daughter, Mary Seton, was one of Mary Queen of Scots' four Marys. It was here that the former Queen took refuge during her flight to Hamilton Palace from imprisonment in Loch Leven Castle in 1568.

Winchburgh nestles among the shale bings, the Union Canal runs through them. This ride demonstrates the amazing beauty hidden away in the midst of this industrial belt. You might think that the name Winchburgh had recent mining connotations referring to the pit-head machinery, but this is not the case. The name means 'the burgh of Winca', who was possibly a Viking, and certainly the village was so called in Wallace's time.

The bing shale is a russet red colour, but has weathered well, elders and rosebay willowherb colonising the lower slopes. This area is the Lothians' equivalent of the Texas oil fields with their 'nodding donkeys'. As with most oilfields the raw material, in this case shale, comes from deep underground, but unlike the method of extraction used in Texas, the Gulf or Iraq, this raw product could not be pumped up. It was won by mining in a very similar way to coal.

By-products were ammonia liquor, crude spirit and gas. The gas went straight back into the retorts to be used for heating. The ammonia was treated with sulphuric acid to form sulphate of ammonia, as crystals for use in agriculture, and the spirit, like the crude oil, went to the refinery. Further down the distillation chain, wax was an important by-product, being made into candles at Broxburn. One claim was that Lothian candle-wax was to be found in wayside shrines all over Russia until the fall of Rasputin. The residue after everything had been extracted was the beautifully tinted rocky flakes, the material of the bings, which you will encounter en route.

Bing shale

Once you have left the canal towpath continue west on the B9080 back towards Linlithgow. This used to be the main road before the M9 motorway was built and it still carries the ageing trappings of a trunk route, but is now a lot quieter, apart from the weekday lorries trundling up to the landfill site a kilometre west of the village. Once these are left behind, there is a marked drop-off in the volume of traffic, not that it was too heavy in any case. Turn right onto the B8046 for Philpstoun just before Threemiletown (presumably so named because of its distance from Linlithgow Palace).

Turn left at Old Philpstoun for Philpstoun itself after you pass the huge bings at Fawnspark, and follow this minor road west roughly parallel to the canal. The road is quiet enough but the towpath seems even more unobtrusive, and it is. When you reach Park Farm you can see the access to the Union Canal at the far side. Rejoin the towpath here and retrace the first 2.5 km back to Linlithgow Station.

Memorial, Winchburgh

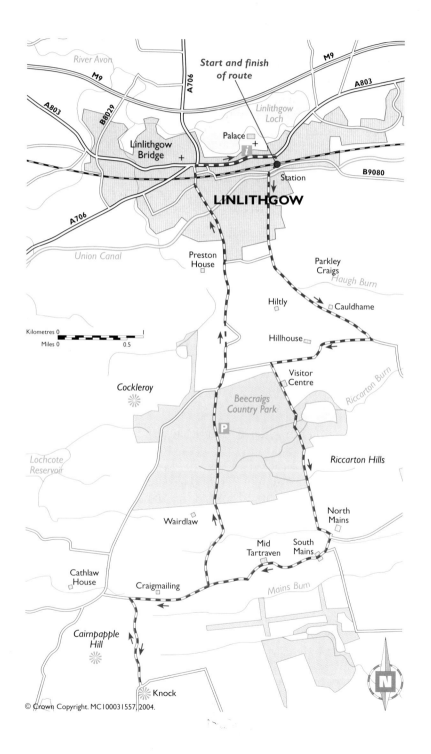

Start and finish of route

River Avon

M9

M9

A803

A706

A803

B8029

Linlithgow Loch

Palace

Linlithgow Bridge

Station

B9080

LINLITHGOW

A706

Union Canal

Preston House

Parkley Craigs

Haugh Burn

Hiltly

Cauldhame

Kilometres 0   1
Miles 0   0.5

Hillhouse

Cockleroy

Visitor Centre

Riccarton Burn

Beecraigs Country Park

P

Lochcote Reservoir

Riccarton Hills

Wairdlaw

North Mains

Cathlaw House

Mid Tartraven

South Mains

Craigmailing

Mains Burn

Cairnpapple Hill

Knock

© Crown Copyright. MC100031557, 2004.

N

BEECRAIGS AND CAIRNPAPPLE HILL

The area around Linlithgow is said to have been where King Arthur fought Picts, Scots and Angles in a series of battles, but then many parts of the British Isles claim to be associated with Arthur. Indeed, the battle of Camlan at which Arthur was eventually slain is said to have taken place near Falkirk. Linlithgow's location midway between Edinburgh and Stirling, with Blackness harbour nearby, meant it was of great strategic importance and the area was known as Scotland's battlefield.

In 1301 Edward I of England built a heavily fortified castle around the existing manor house there. In 1313, after the Wars of Independence, it returned to Scottish control. It continued to suffer badly at the hands of the English, and was twice destroyed by fire. In 1425, King James I had it rebuilt, and the ruin of his castle is what remains today. Before or after you make your cycle run, take some time to explore this beautiful and historic town.

For those not familiar with the Linlithgow area this route will be a total surprise, a tough but staggeringly beautiful ride. This is a hilly, nay a near mountainous tour, but the rewards are enormous. Do not be afraid to walk up the hills, there are views and changes galore. Take your time. The route has been designed with several options to shorten it if the going gets too tough, but persevere as it will only take ten minutes to get back down into Linlithgow.

Start from the Railway Station and follow the same route as in Chapter 1 by turning right on to Station Road and cycling up the first short hill to the Union Canal at Back Station Road.

INFORMATION

Distance: 16.5 km (10.3 miles).

Start and finish: Linlithgow Railway Station.

Map: OS Landranger 65 and Spokes Midlothian Cycle Map.

Terrain: On minor roads and Beecraigs Country Park mountain bike route, a mixture of forest roads and technical single track. This route is extremely hilly throughout.

Refreshments: Wide range of facilities in Linlithgow and restaurant at Beecraigs Country Park.

View from Beecraigs

Here take Manse Road opposite and continue over the canal and uphill once more. From the canal bridge there is a fine view over the town to the Palace, with Linlithgow Loch beyond. You pass a red warning notice proclaiming 'Dark Entry Closed to Motor Vehicles' as you toil uphill, but this is a little road running south of the town and will not affect you. As the Bathgate Hills begin to bite you might notice a pair of splendid stone field gateposts, one of which has fallen. This might be a good excuse to stop and admire the view.

Eventually you reach the junction for the campsite and Beecraigs; turn right, and uphill again! Although the route from here is far from level, by the time you reach the junction above the Visitor Centre the back is broken. It has been a desperate 4.5 km but well worth it.

Beecraigs Country Park is a fantastic development, making the countryside readily accessible. There are red deer at the farm, wild roe deer in the forest, trout to see at the trout farm and many outdoor activities, but today we are cyclists. However if you would like to enjoy the 7 km (4.5 miles) ATB Trail in the south west of the Park you should call at the Visitor Centre for an instruction leaflet. This guides you to the start at Balvormie car park. There are areas of the Park which are off-limits to cyclists, so please respect this. You can of course

Deer, Beecraigs

ride the rest of this route, then do the ATB Trail on the return leg, since you pass Balvormie car park, but you will need a mountain bike as it is a proper off-road course.

Continue downhill from the Visitor Centre past the main car park and entrance to the trout farm, then it is uphill again on a road shaded by an impressive stand of spruce. Eventually you clear the trees, crest the hill and have the relief of freewheeling through open rolling countryside. Follow the signpost west towards Bathgate at South Mains, then straight on past the Balvormie road to Cairnpapple Hill, marked by its transmission mast. This final climb is verging on the alpine, with Armco barriers fringing the road, but the effort is worthwhile, the views are fantastic.

Heron, Beecraigs

As there is such an amazing view from the top, it might be worth carrying your bike up the steps at the summit and tethering it to a fencepost, because the temptation to loiter will be great.

Cairnpapple is an ancient henge site of national importance. It was used at two periods—as a ceremonial Neolithic site around 3000 BC, and as a Bronze Age burial site from around 2000 BC.

Retrace your way back to the Balvormie turn, even diving through the short cut if you've got knobbly tyres, then down a beech-lined avenue, and back towards Linlithgow in a reasonably straight line.

When the road reaches Linlithgow it is called Preston Road which ends at High Street. Here turn right and follow this road into the centre of the town.

Linlithgow Loch is accessed via Water Yett off the High Street. Take something for the wildfowl and this will get you closer to a staggering array of species one normally only sees flying high overhead.

Cairnpapple

The views over the Loch to the Palace and the Abbey Church are breathtaking. Once you have explored the town it will be time to return to the station, which is well signposted from the High Street.

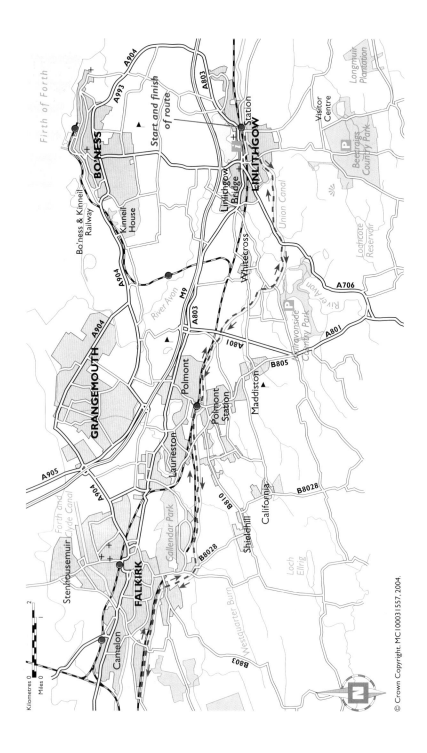

LINLITHGOW TO THE FALKIRK WHEEL

There would be no point in having routes from Linlithgow without having one describing a trip along the Union Canal to see the newest engineering wonder of the world, the Falkirk Wheel, with many interesting places and things to see en route. It has to be admitted, however, that travelling west from Linlithgow you will soon pass out of West Lothian and into the county of Falkirk, and so strictly speaking out of the scope of this book.

Linlithgow means 'the double lake in the hollow', and in this fertile part of the country there would doubtless have existed a settlement from the very earliest times. Indeed there are traces of a Roman settlement in this vicinity: Roman hill-forts have been discovered close to the town and in the eighteenth century a farmer in the area ploughed up an urn containing 300 Roman coins.

After leaving Linlithgow Station, turn right on to Station Road and cycle up the first short hill, at the top of which you will find the Union Canal. On joining the towpath head west. The Union Canal is a contour canal, which means that it follows the natural topography, remaining at the same height throughout its length and therefore not requiring locks. The canal is some 51 km long and was opened in 1822, and so is much younger than the Forth and Clyde Canal, the other Lowland canal.

The route of the canal at Linlithgow travels along the higher land to the south of the town centre, but even so it had to be built on an embankment. In the early 1980s the embankment to the west of the town collapsed over a distance of some 200 m, and this stretch of the canal had to be dammed and de-watered. The canal remained like this for some years until, as part of

Boat meanders along the canal

Avon Aqueduct

the West Lothian Project, British Waterways and the local authorities rebuilt the embankment. A new bridge was also constructed over Preston Road as part of this project which replaced the culvert installed in the 1960s.

After leaving the bounds of Linlithgow, the first place of interest you come to is Woodcockdale Stables, where the horses used for pulling the barges along the canal were kept.

A few kilometres further on you come to the Avon Aqueduct. Spanning the valley on 12 arches, it is some 300 m in length and is the longest and highest Scottish aqueduct. It offers some very fine views over the Avon Valley. This is the first of the three large multi-span structures which were built as part of the original canal. The other two carry the canal across the Almond Valley and the Water of Leith at Slateford.

At the west end of the Avon Aqueduct there is path which leads to a set of steps, at the bottom of which the river Avon flows through the aqueduct. This area is now within Muiravonside Country Park. This country park contains 170 acres of woodlands, parklands and gardens of the Muiravonside Estate, the seat of a branch of the Stirling family who were so influential in shaping the history of Scotland over the last millennium. Attractions include relics of the industrial past, a dovecot, burial ground, summer house and children's farm.

Continue along the towpath for another 5 km to Polmont. This small town is said to be located on the site of a Roman fort. There is no trace left of this ancient fortification, and indeed there is nothing much known about Polmont before the advent of the Edinburgh to Glasgow Railway. Today it is home to many people who work in Edinburgh.

After leaving Polmont the canal winds its way through another 4 km of countryside until it reaches the canal tunnel. En route it passes under the Glen Bridge, which displays a happy face on its eastern keystone and an unhappy face on the western one, and hence is known as 'the Laughin and Greetin Bridge'. It is the largest of the single-arch bridges over the canal.

The canal tunnel, measuring 18 ft wide by 19 ft high, had to be constructed, at great cost,

Author at Falkirk Wheel

through Prospect Hill, because William Forbes, the owner of the adjacent Callendar Estate, would not countenance the canal passing within sight of Callendar House.

The tunnel offers a bit of adventure, as it is 640 m in length and cut through solid rock. On entering, the traveller will find a constant sound of running water and an intense darkness. However, a guard rail runs the entire length. Please do not try to cycle through this tunnel, as the walkway is very narrow. Just walk! It is also a good idea to have a flashlight to see where you are going. Without one it is a walk of faith, but after a while your eyes do get used to the darkness. Waterproof clothing is also beneficial, for some of the running water falls directly on to the walkway. You will have to keep a tight hold of children and dogs, and perhaps parents should think seriously before attempting this route. However, if you are careful nothing is likely to go wrong.

On leaving the tunnel the end of the Union Canal is just over a kilometre away. However, it is worth noting for those of you who wish to travel back to Linlithgow or all the way to Edinburgh, that the access to Falkirk High Station is only a short distance away. So once you have been to see the Wheel you should return to this spot and make your way to the station.

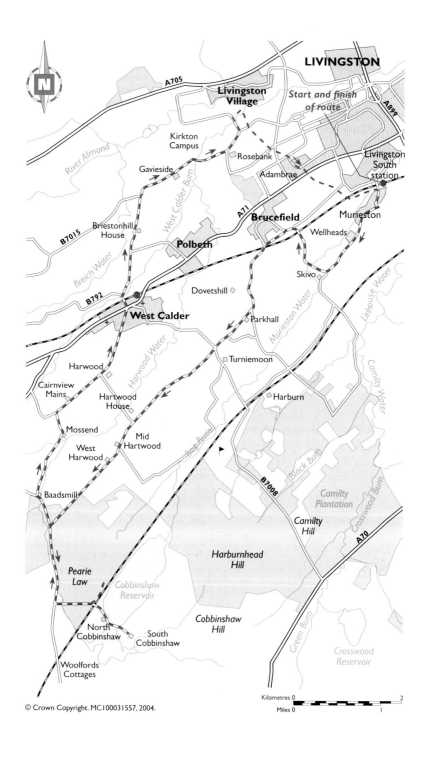

© Crown Copyright. MC100031557, 2004.

LIVINGSTON TO COBBINSHAW RESERVOIR

Livingston was a renowned name long before David Livingstone made it a household word (the surname usually has an e, the place name not). The original village on the River Almond is thought to have been named after Leving, a Flemish family who came to Scotland during Alexander I's reign. It was the seat of the Livingstones, Earls of Linlithgow, probably descendants of the Levings. The estate had a notable botanic garden, and when the house was demolished in 1812, most of the plants were sent to the Physic Garden in Edinburgh, which eventually became the present world famous Royal Botanic Garden.

Back to the present. On leaving Livingston South Station, cycle under the railway to join a series of cycle/footpaths and carry on past Murieston Village Hall to a T-junction. Turn left, and after a few metres there is another junction. Carry straight on here to the Murieston trail alongside the little river of the same name, continuing for approximately 2 km.

More than one path links to the trail in this river valley, but if you keep generally travelling in the same direction you will end up on Murieston Road. On reaching this road turn right and using the pavement on the north side of the road (designated as a cycling pavement), continue for 600 m or so to where the road passes over the railway.

Cross the railway bridge carefully, rejoin the road and soon it sweeps round to the left and then right. At the point where it sweeps to the right there is a minor road which carries straight on. Take this tree-lined road, without

INFORMATION

Distance: 28 km (17.5 miles).

Start and finish: Livingston South Railway Station.

Map: OS Landranger 65, Spokes West Lothian Cycle Map and *Livingston for Cyclists*.

Terrain: Urban cycle tracks and quiet minor roads. Outsde of Livingston the route is undulating with small sections of steeper inclines.

Refreshments: Almondvale Centre and Elm Tree Inn, Bellsquarry.

Oil shale bings

The road to
Cobbinshaw Loch

deviating from it, for 2 km, until you reach the junction with the B7008. Cross this and head straight on. The signpost says Cobbinshaw 4 miles (6 km). This quiet, very pleasant road gently winds its way, through woods and fields, uphill past the National Canine Defence League local headquarters. After 4 km a T-junction is reached. Turn left towards Woolfords, and after 1.5 km you come to the border with South Lanarkshire.

Here the scenery changes dramatically to wild heath land. 200 m further on you come to a junction on the left. Take this even more minor road downhill to where a bridge crosses over the main Edinburgh-Glasgow railway line, just beyond which the road ends at Cobbinshaw Reservoir.

The reservoir supplies water to the City of Edinburgh and also, through a tributary of the river Almond, to the Union Canal. It is on high ground north-west of the Pentland Hills, which form a dramatic backdrop. The area originated as a watering stop for steam trains on the adjacent main line. Relatively few wildfowl use the reservoir, but there is a small goose roost, a few Whooper Swans and a Black-headed Gull colony south of the causeway, and less common species, such as Osprey, visit from time to time.

From the road-end a rough track continues both north and south. Head north and you soon come to the local fishing club with its numbered boats moored nearby. Head south and you arrive at the dam causeway, a nice spot for a picnic on a fine day.

Leave by the route that you came in. Alas, what was an easy run down to the reservoir is a slog on the way back—but not for long. Turn right on to the Woolfords road once again. After returning uphill and re-entering West

Lothian, continue for 1.5 km to the previously visited T-junction, this time carrying straight on.

Soon the road becomes single track and winds downhill to the junction at Baadsmill. Here turn right on to an even narrower single-track road with passing places. Continue

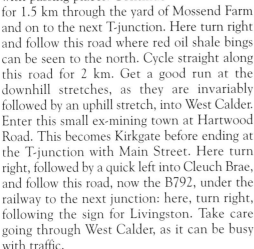

Cobbinshaw Reservoir

for 1.5 km through the yard of Mossend Farm and on to the next T-junction. Here turn right and follow this road where red oil shale bings can be seen to the north. Cycle straight along this road for 2 km. Get a good run at the downhill stretches, as they are invariably followed by an uphill stretch, into West Calder. Enter this small ex-mining town at Hartwood Road. This becomes Kirkgate before ending at the T-junction with Main Street. Here turn right, followed by a quick left into Cleuch Brae, and follow this road, now the B792, under the railway to the next junction: here, turn right, following the sign for Livingston. Take care going through West Calder, as it can be busy with traffic.

Soon you are in open country once again, but not for long, as after 3.5 km Livingston is reached at Simpson Parkway. Here follow the pavement cycle track on the north side of this road to the underpass. Carry on through the underpass, and after 200 m turn right on to the Waverley Path and head south. Stay on this path for 750 m to where it then heads east to the perimeter of Dedridge Quarry Pond. Here turn right, soon passing through an underpass at Dedridge West, then head right and quickly left under the A71. From here go straight through Bankton Mains Park and then left under Murieston West, then turn right and follow the path which soon goes under the railway. Here the route should look familiar as it was part of the outward journey. So turn left and retrace the path to the station.

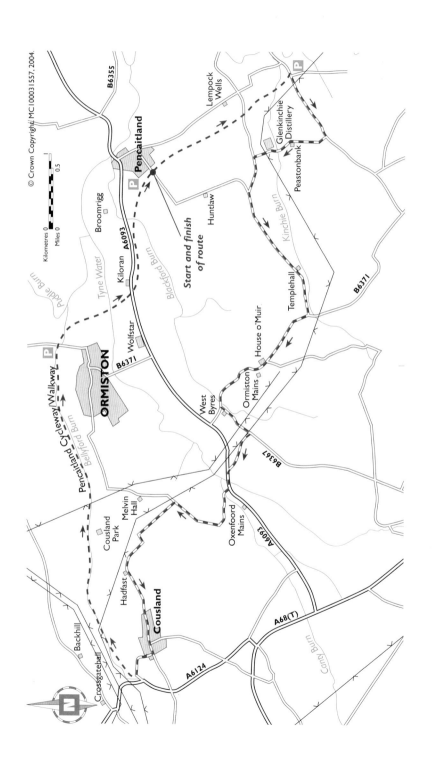

PENCAITLAND RAILWAY

This is a circular tour of the former East Lothian coalfield, something totally missed by motorists but afforded to cyclists by the Pencaitland Railway Path. Railways, cutting through in fairly straight lines, give a unique view of the countryside. In the days of the steam train they were noted havens for wildlife. Occasional trackside fires caused by errant sparks would blight a stretch for a time, but the vegetation soon recovered, growing back with tremendous vigour.

Nowadays this trackside is actively managed to encourage wildlife, probably more varied than ever due to its many years of abandonment. Over 90 bird species have been recorded. You won't see them all in one day; however, even before leaving the car park you will probably notice blue-tits, coal-tits, yellowhammers and the inevitable sparrows haunting the grain silos. Once onto the old track bed you will see blackbirds scratching among the fallen leaves, and hawks on a high perch waiting for their next meal. Mice and voles are plentiful, if not immediately obvious. You will be well advised to watch for recent hazardous holes dug by rabbits or even badgers. Spring flowers include apple and cherry blossom, gorse, broom, willow and rowan, while later in the year you may find wild strawberries and incredible banks of purple rosebay willowherb between the bridges near Milton House.

This line closed in 1964 with the closure of the last mine in the area. Passenger services had already been withdrawn in 1933. Traditionally the railway was the main thoroughfare in mining areas. Since it was usually the most direct line of communication, every railway had a path alongside, used by

INFORMATION

Distance: 22 km (13.5 miles).

Start and finish: Site of Pencaitland Station.

Map: OS Landranger 66 and Spokes East Lothian Cycle Map.

Terrain: Nearly half of the route, 9.1 km (5.7 miles) is on railway path, all of which is good when dry, but in wet conditions can provide some soft strenuous stretches suitable only for mountain bikes. The remainder of the route is on minor roads which are fairly quiet.

Refreshments: None en route.

The author rides the route again

Old cottage,
new technology

both local pedestrians and cyclists. So you will see that a shared facility is nothing new, but please treat other users with due consideration.

The car park at the start of the ride is beside the huge grain silos at the west end of Pencaitland village, south of the A6093 road. Access is via a bumpy road down the side of the silo site, the entrance being marked by a blue cycleway fingerpost sign announcing Ormiston 2 Saltoun 2.

Pencaitland's name, meaning 'knoll of the narrow valley', perfectly describes its location in the Tyne Valley, an area with rich agricultural land.

Begin by heading south-east towards Saltoun. Though you could reasonably expect the railway to be level, a little gradient post indicates a 1 in 50 climb to start. Opposite the last bungalow of Pencaitland a tombstone plaque marks the site of the most south-easterly mine in the Haddington area. Nothing now remains. Were it not for this reminder you would never think this place had been anything other than the vast field it now is.

The cycleway continues into a sometimes damp cutting, then suddenly you reach the end of the line at Saltoun Station. Turn right on to the minor road and carry on up the hill past beech hedges. Take the first right again and carry on for 500m to the little hamlet of Peastonbank. At the far end of this stands Glenkinchie Distillery, with its chimney like the neck of a bottle. The home of the fine lowland malt takes its name and its water from the Kinchie Burn, which it was founded in 1824. If you pass between 0930 and 1600, Monday to Friday, you may be tempted to join a guided tour!

After passing the distillery, turn left at the next junction and follow this road for almost 3 km to where it joins the B6371. Turn right here and carry on for a further 2 km to West Byres. Here turn left onto a very narrow road and then right on to the B6367 before coming to the junction of the A6093. Here turn left and then take the first right, staying on this busy main road for only 100 m before joining another

Glenkinchie Distillery

minor road. The road to Cousland is signposted on the left once you are beyond Airfield road end, and is very steep. This is a good time to dismount with the excuse of admiring the countryside. Once through the small village of Cousland turn right and continue downhill to the A6124. Turn right and continue for 500 m to where the railway path begins.

Another blue fingerpost points the way to Pencaitland. This is Crossgatehall. Initially the path is well surfaced but narrows as you progress. Then it comes into sight: the pitheap, the biggest visible reminder of the coalfield. More tombstones record the sites of the pits. You'll probably be surprised how close together they lie. One reads: 'Oxenford Pit (Ormiston Coal Co.) Sunk 1907 re-sunk 1909 abandoned 1932. Output before closure 250/300 tons a day. Smeaton 2.6 miles.' The cycleway passes to the north of Ormiston, a village by the River Tyne with a population of around 2,000. Designed in 1735 as a model farming village by John Cockburn, its broad, tree-lined main street still reflects his architectural vision. About a mile further south stands the Cockburn family seat, Ormiston House, built in 1745. In 1545, at the much older house (now restored) nearby, George Wishart was arrested on the instructions of Cardinal Beaton and taken to St Andrews to be burned at the stake.

Stone commemorating the Oxenford pit

Continue to the A6093 again and cross it with care. Thereafter it is but a short distance back to where the route began.

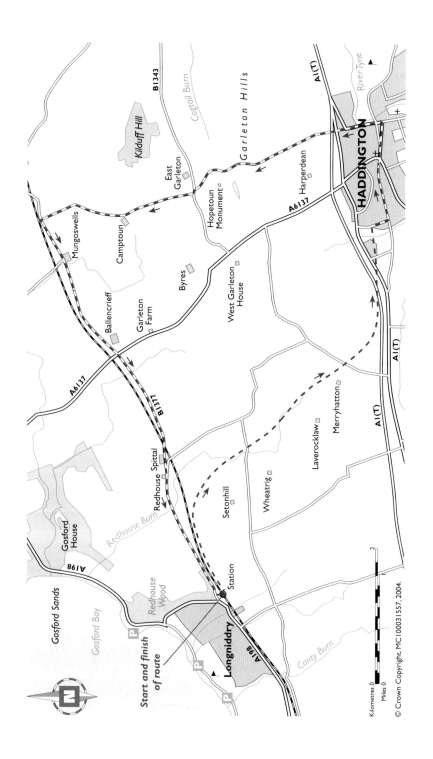

© Crown Copyright. MC100031557. 2004.

LONGNIDDRY TO HADDINGTON

The route begins at Longniddry Station, using the Longniddry to Haddington off-road cycle path which starts on the B1377 just after the roundabout at Lyars Road.

The railway path swings inland for a little over 6 km towards Haddington, and you are in the depths of the country within minutes. Unlike most railway paths, which are coaly black, this one is red for most of its length, in keeping with the surrounding countryside.

Eventually you become aware of the A1 traffic roar, but at this stage you go under the bypass and into the outskirts of Haddington, where a Toucan crossing awaits to guide you safely onto the final stretch of track.

This route ends at Alderston Road. Turn right and follow this to its end where it joins West Road (B6471). Turn left here, and continue the short distance to the town centre. Today this beautiful market town is once more the county town of East Lothian. There are many interesting places to see and it is well worth taking some time to look around. Don't worry about parking your bikes, as there are plenty of parking stands dotted around the town.

Haddington, situated in the Tyne valley, was created a Royal Burgh by King David I. David's grandson, William, who succeeded Malcolm VI as king of Scotland, had a palace built in Haddington and it was there that Alexander II was born in 1214.

In 1386 the town was put to the torch by Edward III, who comprehensively laid waste to it including the beautiful church built by monks of the Franciscan order to rival the

INFORMATION

Distance: 22 km (13.5 miles). Circular route.

Map: OS Landranger, sheet 66, and Spokes East Lothian Cycle Map.

Start and finish: Longniddry Railway Station.

Terrain: Cycle route and minor roads. Undulating with stretches of steeper hills.

Refreshments: Places in Longniddry and Haddington.

Haddington

Looking over to the
East Lothian coast

Abbey at Newbattle. This church, because of its remarkable beauty, was known as the Lamp of Lothian. This name was also given to the church of St Mary built later to replace the Abbey church. This church, itself a ruin until recently, has been completely restored by the Lamp of Lothian Trust.

In 1598, Haddington was again burned, the calamity having been caused through the carelessness of a maidservant who placed a screen covered with clothes too near a fireplace during the night, setting the house on fire. This fire quickly spread, destroying many buildings in its wake. As a result of this the local magistrate decreed that henceforth the town crier should tour the town during the winter evenings, warning the people to guard against fire. The ceremony got the name of 'Coal an' Can'le', at which the following verses were recited by the crier.

A' guid man's servants where'er ye be,
Keep coal an' can'le for charitie!
Baith in your kitchen an' your ha',
Keep weel your fires whate'er befa'!

In bakehouse, brewhouse, barn and byre,
I warn ye a' keep weel your fire!
For oftentimes a little spark
Brings mony hands to meikle wark!

Ye nourrices that hae bairns to keep,
See that ye fa' nae o'er sound asleep,
For losing o' your guid renoun,
An' banishing o' this barrous toun.

'Tis, for your sakes that I do cry:
Tak warning by your neighbour's bye!

At Giffordgate in the east end of the town is the place where John Knox, one of the orchestrators of the Reformation in Scotland, was born between 1505 and 1515 (the date is disputed by historians).

Hopetoun Monument

The route continues down Market Street, left into Hardgate and then straight on to Dunbar Road where it continues to Haldane Avenue. Here turn right and follow the cycle lane to the roundabout, where you should use the pavement to circumnavigate this double roundabout system. Follow the minor road signposted for Drem. After an initial steep and lengthy incline, gaining more than one hundred metres in elevation in less than two kilometres, the road begins to drop down towards the coast, with beautiful views of the surrounding countryside stretching as far as Edinburgh in the west and Berwick Law in the east. Closer there is a view of the chimney-shaped Hopetoun monument, erected in memory of the fourth Earl of Haddington. Carry straight on at the split road junction, but before doing so, if you deviate a few metres to the right, you will get a good view of the ruins of Garleton Castle, birthplace of Sir David Lindsay, the famous sixteenth century playwright. As you run downhill just after Campstoun you will pass the entrance to the site of an Iron Age fort called the Chesters to the east of the road. The fort is well preserved, with an elaborate system of ramparts and ditches. This site is run by Historic Scotland and is well worth seeing.

Garleton Castle

Returning to the route, continue to the T-junction with the B1377 where a left turn is made. Follow this road in a westerly direction for 6 km back to Longniddry.

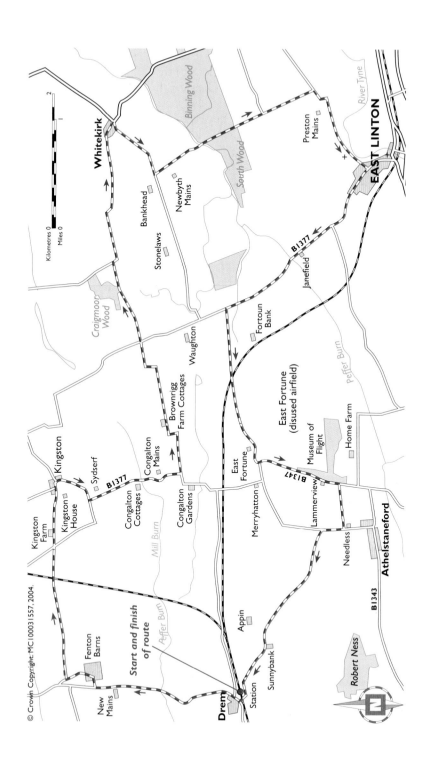

© Crown Copyright MC100031557, 2004.

Kilometres 0
Miles 0

Whitekirk

Binning Wood

South Wood

River Tyne

EAST LINTON

Preston Mains

Bankhead

Newbyth Mains

Stonelaws

Craigmoor Wood

B1377

Janefield

Fortoun Bank

Waughton

Brownrigg Farm Cottages

Kingston

Sydserf

B1377

Congalton Cottages

Congalton Mains

Mill Burn

Congalton Gardens

East Fortune

East Fortune (disused airfield)

Museum of Flight

Home Farm

Peffer Burn

Kingston Farm

Kingston House

Merryhatton

Lammerview

B1347

Athelstaneford

Needless

Fenton Barns

Start and finish of route

Peffer Burn

Appin

Sunnybank

Drem

Station

New Mains

B1343

Robert Ness

DREM TO EAST LINTON

Drem is a small attractive village surrounded by fertile land close to the ancient hill fort called the Chesters. It stands on the East Coast main line to England, with a branch line to North Berwick. An airfield established here during World War I became a significant base during World War II. From here fighter planes fought bravely against German bombers attacking the naval base at Rosyth. A lighting system was pioneered at RAF Drem enabling aircraft to take off and land in bad weather and at night, and was named after the base.

On leaving the station, turn right and follow the B1345 in the direction of Dirleton. After 2.5 km turn right following the minor road to Fenton Barns. Fenton Barns was part of RAF Drem up to the end of World War II. Its historic buildings are now used as galleries, work studios and a coffee house. After Fenton Barns, continue to a T-junction on the right: turn right here and follow this road to Kingston. Here turn right on to the B1347 and follow this road for 2 km to a T-junction. Turn left and carry on along this road for 4 km to Whitekirk. Whitekirk was a renowned place of pilgrimage in the middle ages. The existing church is largely fifteenth century. It was restored on two occasions, once in 1885 and again in 1913 after being burned by suffragettes. At this pleasant little village, at the telephone box just a few metres short of the junction with the A198, there is a minor road off to the right. Take this for a kilometre and then turn left on to another minor road signposted for East Linton.

This tree-lined road is dead straight along its 2 km length and offers good shelter from the heat of the sun or, perhaps

INFORMATION

Distance: 26 km (16.3 miles). Circular route.

Map: OS Landranger, sheets 66 and 67, and Spokes East Lothian Cycle Map.

Start and finish: Drem Railway Station.

Terrain: Minor roads. This route is fairly flat with undulating stretches. It is not difficult.

Refreshments: Places in East Linton.

Cottages at Drem

Rocket at the Museum of Flight

more likely, the rain. It ends at a T-junction with the B1407 where you turn right. Soon you reach the town of East Linton and a few metres further you come to the access road into Preston Mill, one of the oldest mechanically intact water-driven mills in Scotland. There is thought to have been a mill here since the twelfth century, although the current buildings, with their attractive red pantiles, date from the seventeenth and eighteenth centuries. In 1760 Andrew Meikle installed the first ever cast-iron mill-wheel, probably made at the Carron Iron Works. He also invented the threshing machine.

The mill, with its conical-roofed kiln for drying the corn and millpond with many ducks and geese, is a wonderful sight and an idyllic place to spend some time. Visitors can see the mill operating and an exhibition on its history and the life of a miller.

The attractive village of East Linton, the centre of which is reached soon after leaving the mill, is also a good place to tarry a while. Its buildings include the eighteenth-century Prestonkirk parish church, with a remarkable thirteenth-century chancel and burial site of the Smeaton family. A sixteenth-century bridge spans the River Tyne over a gorge in the centre of the village. This bridge was on the Edinburgh-London road, and an important crossing point.

Leave the village the way you entered it, but this time carry straight on, following the B1377 all the way back to Drem if you wish. However, after 6 km you reach the B1347 on the left, which leads after less than a kilometre to the Museum of Flight at East Fortune. This is part of the National Museums of Scotland and was opened in 1975 on what had been a disused RAF airfield. The airfield was established in 1915 as a Royal Naval Air Station, to defend

Edinburgh and the Forth Bridge from attack by German airships. After the war it saw an historic flight when the R34 airship, constructed by the Beardmore Engineering Company of Inchinnan, made a double crossing of the Atlantic. It left East Fortune on 2 July 1919 and landed on Long Island, New York, on 6 July, returning to complete the journey in Lincolnshire on 13 July. After operating as a support station for the nearby RAF Drem, the airfield then became a training base.

Preston Mill

Today, the museum displays around 50 aircraft, the largest being an Avro Vulcan bomber, and the oldest a Hawk Glider, built by Percy Pilcher in 1896, together with a vast amount of aeronautical equipment and archives in two hangar-galleries. After leaving the museum, return to the B1377 to complete the journey to Drem. Or turn left at the end of the museum access road on to the B1347 and head south for a kilometre, then turn right on to the minor road signposted for Athelstaneford.

The village of Athelstaneford takes its name from the legendary ninth-century battle between the Saxon King Athelstane and the Pictish King Hungus. The Scottish Flag Heritage Centre in the village commemorates the battle, during which the Cross of St Andrew appeared in the sky, inspiring the Picts to defeat their enemy. After this it became their emblem, and later when Scotland was united it became the national flag. Athelstaneford, built in the late eighteenth century by Sir David Kinloch of Gilmerton, is a fine example of a model village. He wanted to improve the housing conditions of local farmworkers, and provided well-proportioned housing and a sizeable garden for a nominal rent. A weaving industry was established in the village, producing a striped cloth. After visiting the village, travel north on the B1343 for about 500 m, then bear left on to the minor road signposted for Drem.

The Drover's Inn, East Linton

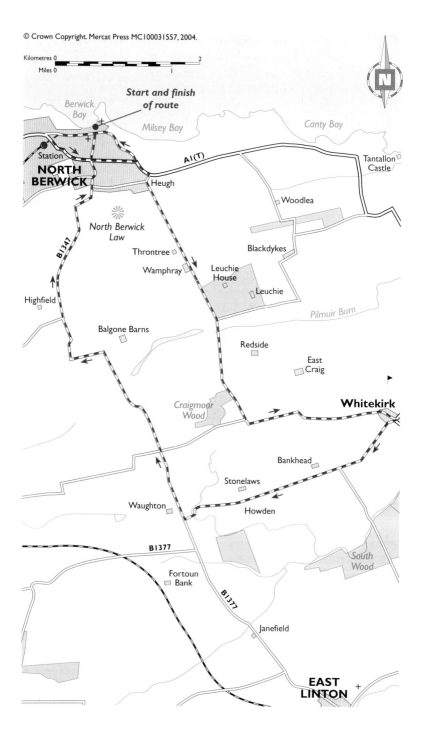

© Crown Copyright. Mercat Press MC100031557, 2004.

NORTH BERWICK TO WHITEKIRK

The first and latter stages of this ride are dominated by Berwick Law, at 187 m (614 feet) one of the most prominent landmarks in East Lothian. The climb to the top is rewarded by an incredible panoramic view of the Fife coastline, the Firth of Forth and the Lothians. A memorial plate on the summit guides your eye and helps you to identify all the islands and the surrounding mountain ranges, from the snow-topped Grampians to the Ochil Hills, the Pentlands, Moorfoots and the Lammermuirs. East and West Lomond, across the Firth in Fife, seem very close, but in fact are 38 km away.

Many of the great individual mountains are indicated too—Glas Maol, 100 km to the north, Ben Vorlich, 9 km further and Ben Lomond, the most southerly of the Munros, an incredible 121 km to the west. However, visibility would need to be first-class for that sighting.

Not surprisingly there is evidence of human occupation on the Law from the Iron Age, through the Roman period and possibly as late as the Middle Ages. There are some historic finds in North Berwick museum. More recent evidence can still be seen. The old ruin near the summit is the remains of a look-out built in 1803 when Napoleon was threatening to invade Britain, and there are the famous whale's jawbones. The present set was erected in 1936, but the first were carried to the top in 1709.

Berwick Law is a good example of the geological feature known as 'crag and tail', formed by the movement of an ice sheet which covered this area during the last Ice Age.

INFORMATION

Distance: 16 km (10 miles). Circular route.

Start and finish: North Berwick Station.

Map: OS Landranger, sheets 66 and 67, and Spokes East Lothian Cycle Map.

Terrain: Minor Roads. Undulating route with short steep hills.

Refreshments: None en route. Full facilities in North Berwick.

Whale jaw bones on Berwick Law

Hay bales

The ascent on foot to the summit will put you on top of the crag; the crossing of the tail by bike begins on the outskirts of North Berwick and tops out at Heugh Farm.

Leave the station and turn right along Station Road, then left and join Marmion Crescent. Take the first right into Clifford Road which later becomes St Baldred's Road. Continue without deviation to the junction with Dunbar Road and turn right. Here you are confronted with the classic view of the Law and the whalebone arch. Climb up past the rugby club, then straight on at the roundabout into Heugh Brae, following the sign for East Linton, and up over the 'tail' towards Leuchie House, a convent at the little settlement of Wamphray. The hill you encounter is a short sharp shock so early in the ride, but the height gain puts you into new undulating country and that is the serious climbing finished for the outward leg.

Continue along this interesting road where, on my last trip, three mallard flew out of the wood on the right, then a pair of heron lifted from the tiny stream at the bottom of a hill. Hidden away unseen in the grounds of Balgone House, which was built as a nunnery in the fifteenth century, there are a couple of large ponds, no doubt the source of good water and food for the birds.

Later the road turns east towards Whitekirk. The skyline then presents the Lammermuir Hills and the red roofs of Whitekirk. The village seems to have been hewn out of the solid rock. Some of the cottages even have their back gardens in the old quarry. You turn right at the T-junction by the telephone kiosk in the village, but take the time for a detour of 40 metres along to St Mary's, the historic parish church of Whitekirk and Tyninghame. It is an impressive old building.

Bass Rock

Traprain Law, another volcanic outcrop, dominates the view as you ride west towards Waughton. Pheasants wandered idly out into the road as I arrived at Angus Wood, a hazardous thing to do in front of a descending cyclist, but there were no fatalities on either side. Turn north at the junction near Waughton and watch out for other traffic. The road now rises stiffly again to crest the ridge near the ruined Waughton Castle. Turn left and immediately right, then up again towards North Berwick. The ruined castle at Waughton is of fourteenth century construction, with only part of one wing surviving. In 1536 it was sacked by the English during the 'Rough Wooing' of Henry VIII.

Rocky outcrops in many of the fields underline the nature of the land, but the richness is there for all to see. The ruined windmill above Balgone Barns looks like some kind of giant chimney, then suddenly the Law monopolises the horizon again. Soon you are close enough to see the white triangulation pillar on the top. The Firth of Forth reappears, then the riding is steadily downhill to the outskirts of North Berwick, entering the town at Haddington Road which soon becomes Law Road. Follow this road all the way to High Street. Park your bike and enjoy the many amenities of this very pleasant town. All that remains is to weave your way back to the station.

Yachts in the harbour, North Berwick

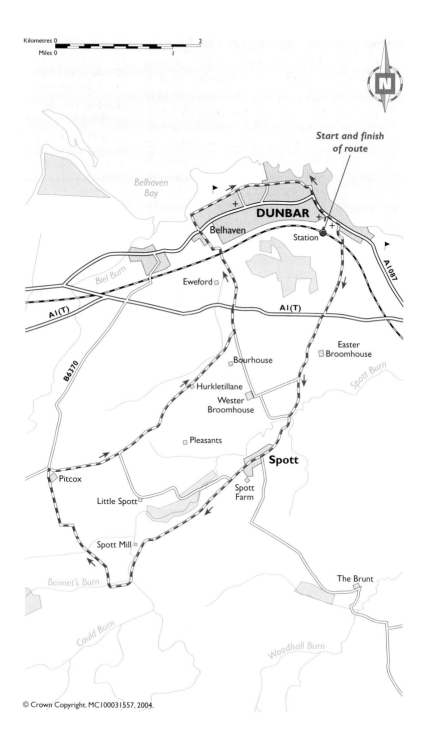

Start and finish of route

DUNBAR TO SPOTT

Red sandstone dominates this ride. There are red soils throughout the Lothians and the Borders, but Dunbar is reddest of all—according to the historian George Scott-Moncrieff, 'red as the guts of men'. Dunbar is an ancient place which owes its origins to a natural harbour. This is overlooked by Dunbar Castle standing on a defensible rock, a promontory, above the North Sea. The castle is thought to have been first built by the Northumbrians, but later it was given to the first Earl of Dunbar in 1070 by Malcolm Canmore. Two centuries later, a convent and priory were established by Patrick, fifth Earl of Dunbar. The ninth Earl founded Scotland's first collegiate church here in 1342. In 1445 Dunbar became a royal burgh, and ten years later its castle was forfeited to the Crown. Frequently destroyed and then re-fortified, the castle was visited by Mary Queen of Scots in 1566 after the murder of David Riccio, and a year later was finally demolished by Regent Moray.

The town has been a fishing and trading port for several centuries. Its harbour was rebuilt in 1650 with a grant of £300 from Oliver Cromwell, whose troops had taken the town in battle. During the eighteenth century Dunbar grew as an industrial centre, with whaling, distilling, brewing and the manufacture of textiles. In the late nineteenth century, it developed as a holiday resort with fine golf courses. Dunbar was the birthplace of the conservationist John Muir (1838–1914), whose achievements are remembered at his birthplace, the John Muir Centre, and in the naming of a coastal country park designated nearby in 1982.

INFORMATION

Distance: 18 km (11 miles). Circular route.

Start and finish: Dunbar Railway Station.

Map: OS Landranger, sheet 67, and Spokes East Lothian Cycle Map.

Terrain: Minor roads. Undulating route with short steeper hills.

Refreshments: Full range of facilities in Dunbar, nothing elsewhere on the route.

The route

View over Dunbar harbour

Leave the station, head up Station Road and turn left on to Countess Road, and then immediately right into Abbey Road. Turn right once again into the latter part of High Street and then straight on to Queens Road. After about 250 m turn right on to Spott Road and carry on for a kilometre, under the railway, to the main A1 road, which must be crossed with care. However, to help with this there has been provision made for cyclists to use the adjacent footways, and there are refuge islands in the middle of the carriageway.

A signpost tells you Spott is a distance away, but what it does not impart is that it is uphill. The site of the first Battle of Dunbar in 1296 is passed on the right hand side of the road. This is where the Scots were defeated by Edward I after John Balliol had renounced his allegiance to England.

Continue over Doon Bridge at Canongate and through the village of Spott, after which the road climbs alongside Spott Dod and the Chesters, where there are the remains of an Iron Age fort. This is the most severe climb of the route. There are great views over much of East Lothian as you approach the hills of Lothian Edge. Depth posts give warning of the water level at the little ford beyond Spott Mill, the northern flanks of the Lammermuir Hills providing great flood potential, but most of the year you will not even splash your feet. In case of doubt use the adjacent bridge.

Turn right at the T-junction, across Bennet's Burn via a bridge and up the last hill of any consequence. As we cycled the route the newly ploughed fields were maroon in the afternoon sun and there was silent rejoicing that the wind was now at our backs. The views jump out and present themselves as you crest the hill, from Dunbar to North Berwick laid out like a map before you as you make the descent to Pitcox. We recorded forty-one miles per hour with the help of the wind, but do not forget you need to turn right at the junction. Several of the fields between Pitcox and Belhaven have no hedge or wall, which gives a pleasant open feel to the countryside, and there was the smell of neeps and freshly turned soil on more than one occasion.

Museum, Dunbar

Near Bowerhouse, guardian geese stretched their necks in defiance and it is worth slowing to admire the lodge as you ride past. Just before the A1 is reached, you will see a round sign depicting a pedestrian and a cyclist. This sign invites you to turn left through a gate to join a path on the other side, which carries on under the busy main road before joining a parallel road beyond. Cross this much quieter road on to a minor road and continue for a kilometre to the bridge under the railway. After this, the road turns at right angles, first left, then right, so take care here. Continue past Belhaven Hospital and the Brewery to the junction with Edinburgh Road, and continue straight across into Shore Road. Carry on to the junction with Back Road and turn right. This road continues through three name changes, and alongside Winterfield Golf Course, before arriving at the junction with Victoria Street and High Street. The first takes you on to the harbour area, the second through the town and back to the station. If the tide is right you can finish with a paddle in the bay!

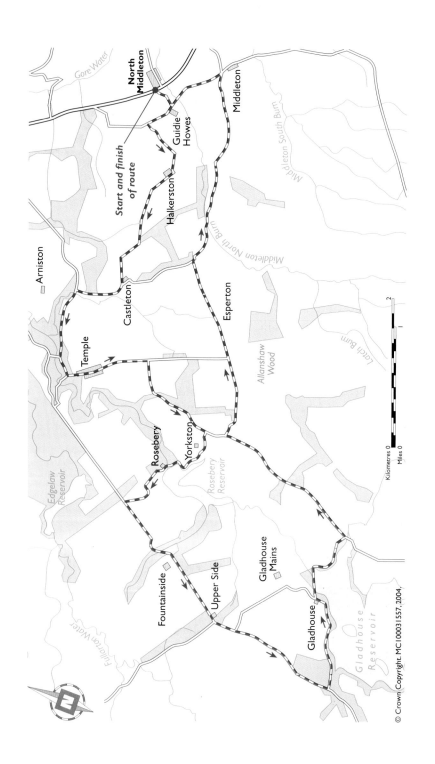

Start and finish of route

North Middleton
Guidie Howes
Halkerston
Middleton
Arniston
Castleton
Esperton
Temple
Rosebery
Yorkston
Allanshaw Wood
Gladhouse Mains
Fountainside
Upper Side
Gladhouse
Gore Water
Edgelaw Reservoir
Fullarton Water
Rosebery Reservoir
Gladhouse Reservoir
Middleton North Burn
Middleton South Burn
Larch Burn

Kilometres 0   1   2
Miles 0

© Crown Copyright. MC100031557, 2004.

MOORFOOT RESERVOIRS

This ride is long and very hilly, but the rewards are high. Even on a bitterly cold day in early January it was a great tour, albeit with a certain amount of excitement generated by sheets of ice covering the entire road in a couple of places! Invariably you find reservoirs in high and remote places. Gladhouse and Rosebery, nestling beneath the Moorfoot Hills, are no exception. The Moorfoot, or Muirfoot, Hills dominate the southern skyline of the tour, and should you look down on this area from their heights it would seem reasonably flat. This is far from the truth, as locally the ground rises and falls very sharply on occasions. Do not be put off by the heights on the map. The ride starts 200 m above sea level. Depart south-west towards the lime works, go right up the hill at Guildie Howes and first left up an even steeper hill towards Halkerston. The tarmac of this sustained hill is quite rough and the gradient is taxing. Look towards the Pentlands which don't seem so high now, the main reason being you are now 260 m above sea level. As we climbed an enormous flock of wood-pigeon, 300 or more, lifted off the winter neeps.

Continue to the B6372, but take time to inspect the ornate southern gate of Arniston, its pillars featuring heraldic beasts.

The mansion house of Arniston was built in the eighteenth century by John Adam, brother of the more famous Robert, to a design by their father William Adam. Between them, the brothers designed and built many great Scottish buildings, including parts of the New Town of Edinburgh.

INFORMATION

Distance: 26 km (16 miles). Circular route.

Start and finish: North Middleton, old road SW of A7(T). There is more room on the far side of the A7, but exercise great care crossing the main road.

Map: OS Landranger, sheet 66, and Spokes Midlothian Cycle Map.

Terrain: Quiet minor roads, some single track. Very hilly.

Refreshments: None en route. Middleton Inn at start/finish, pub grub.

Rosebery Reservoir from on high

Heraldic beast at Arniston

The house is owned by the Dundas family, one of the most powerful legal and political families in Scotland for more than 300 years, and contains a fine collection of portraits by Henry Raeburn and Allan Ramsay. The house is open to the public in April, May and June.

Once you are finished at the house carry on along the B6372 to Braidwood Bridge, at which point head straight on, taking the minor road to Temple.

Allow yourself time for a short diversion onto Braidwood Bridge, as it will also give you a breather before the long pull up through Temple. The noise of the weir on the downstream side strikes one immediately. Take your time up the hill through Temple. The cottage architecture is worth a look, and you may notice the little school hidden away behind the main street. Carry on over the top of the hill and beyond the dip turn right at the sign for Rosebery, alas to face another climb. You turn right for Rosebery Reservoir before the hilltop cottages with their tiny coal-houses at the opposite side of the road, and weave down through Yorkston farm.

The first sight of the reservoir you get is the tip of the eastern arm, where we saw a pair of swans paddling in the icy water. Then an ever-tightening right hand bend takes you down onto the dam, where it is imperative you stop and admire this charming place. The grounds are beautifully kept, a raft of mallard bobbed nearby as we passed and a remarkable pattern formed as the water lapped over the spillway. Rosebery is not big, but the keeper once saw a roe deer stag swim all the way across the widest part, come ashore, leap the fence and quietly walk off up the road totally unconcerned. Quite a feat!

Continue to the B6372, turn left and carry on past Fountainside, following the sign for

Gladhouse onto a lesser road. Old limekilns provide roadside interest along the way. Toxsidehill (290m) is the highest point on your route, but do not get carried away on the downhill because you turn left at the bottom for Gladhouse Reservoir.

Route enters a wood

Even in the depth of winter Gladhouse is a bonnie place. With a little weak sun the water comes alive. There are two car parks with by high banks which make excellent sites for a break, but when we visited the wind was freshening and it was a case of dining standing up! A sheet of ice covered the water stretching up to the dam wall, where there were a few centimetres of clear water.

Now starts the run for home—narrow roads all the way, initially north past Howburn, set some distance back across the fields. Almost 2 km further on turn right on the road past Outerston and continue for 3 km, then turn right again. Carry on past a series of disused quarries to Middleton. There is an unusual brick bridge across the Middleton North Burn and a ruinous and overgrown limestone quarry building as you climb the hill beyond. As you reach the top of the hill you will see that limestone extraction still going on. A huge gorge has been dug here over the years, and you get a good impression here of the scale of the operation. At Middleton crossroads turn left to pass the modern kilns and retrace your way to the car park.

Wind farm on faraway Dun Law

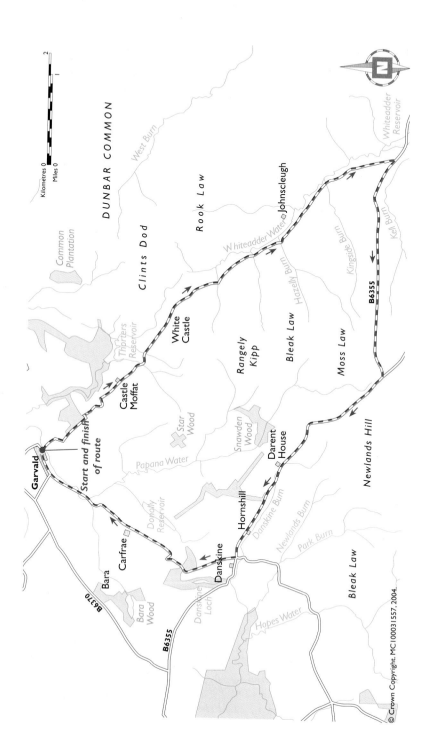

THE ROOF OF LOTHIAN

Much of the Lothians is very hilly, but this route reaches the heights. It is a tough ride up to the highest metalled road in the Lammermuir Hills, 433 m (1420 feet) on Wanside Rig.

The picturesque village of Garvald lies 8 km south-east of Haddington and 6.5 km south of East Linton between the Papana Water and the Lammermuir Hills. The village church, rebuilt in 1829, dates from the twelfth century, and there are a number of listed eighteenth and nineteenth-century buildings including the former school and schoolhouse.

Depart east-north-east past the Garvald Hotel, heading around the bend and up the hill towards Priestlaw, which, if you cannot find it on your map, is the farm on the far side of the Whiteadder Reservoir.

There are breaks in the climbing, but not many, so set a reasonable pace and do not be too proud to get off and walk if the going gets too tough. Walking gives you even more time to observe your surroundings, and there is plenty to absorb. Initially the roadside is lined with holly hedges, which is unusual considering how slowly holly grows. Soon you come to an impressive red stone lodge at the entrance to Nunraw, then at the top of the hill there is one of the most modern monasteries in the land, Sancta Maria Abbey. Known locally as Nunraw, it is the only Cistercian monastery in Scotland, founded from the mother house of Rosecrea, in Ireland. Construction began in 1954 and it took the monks fifteen years to build with plenty of volunteer help. 'Fords 2 miles and 3 miles' is the warning at the bottom of

INFORMATION

Distance: 25 km (15.5 miles). Circular route.

Start and finish: Garvald Church car park.

Map: OS Landranger, sheet 67, and Spokes East Lothian Cycle Map.

Terrain: Minor roads. Exceptionally hilly.

Refreshments: None en route.

Garvald Church

Storm clouds over
Whiteadder Reservoir

the hill beyond the abbey, and on the next climb you are confronted by castellated walls. This turns out to be Castle Moffat, a farm. The trees west of the road revel in the title of the Clartydut Strip and you may glimpse the tiny Thorters Reservoir as you start to climb again. The road ahead snakes its way, with ever-increasing severity, towards the Reservoir. The countryside here is more like the Isle of Skye than Lothian. You may even be struck by a sudden interest in Iron Age forts at White Castle, and who could blame you, but cresting the hill just beyond, you will see that this is the highest point of the route at 345 m (1132 feet). White Castle, right next to the road, stands on an outcrop on the northern edge of the Lammermuir Hills. Circular in shape, with two entrances, it is defended to the south by three impressive ramparts. These probably continued right around the hill, but may have been lost to the north due to landslip, since there is such a steep slope. By the roadside is an information board with details of the site and an artist's impression of how it may have looked.

Once you have crossed the highest point on this stretch of road you enter a different world. The road undulates, but falls more than it climbs, and there are fairly frequent cattle-grids. The road now sweeps high above the Whiteadder Burn giving an elevated and exhilarating ride. Johnscleugh comes into view, a classic hill farm perched on a knoll above the river. Finally you can see the northern arm of the Whiteadder Reservoir and the causeway creating the lesser loch. This is the place for lunch, for if it is a bleak day, no matter which way the wind blows, you can find shelter. The ride to the causeway takes no time at all. As we arrived there were mallard and gorgeous little tufted ducks on the water and an aerial mock battle taking place between a crow and a buzzard. I mused whether the bird of prey had a sense of humour, as it was making a thorough nuisance of itself and seemed greatly to enjoy the pursuit of the crow.

Sancta Maria Abbey

Lunch over, it is back up the little hill and straight on towards Gifford on the B6355. The wide road at the reservoir becomes a narrow single carriageway at the crest of the rise, then contours gently around the hill, past a large railway goods van. The climbing starts again in earnest at a line of gnarled noble beeches which seem out of place here. The hill does not actually go on for ever, it just seems that way. Just as it starts to fall, as inevitably it must, you reach a junction where you must turn left towards Longformacus to reach the Roof of Lothian. The highest point, 433 m above sea level, is only 350 m along the road. There is nothing to mark it, only you will know when you get there! A cheeky red grouse seemed to be the guardian of the summit as it popped out, crying 'back, back, back'. So take his advice and turn back to the road junction, but this time carry straight on. In fact better views are afforded on the road towards Gifford. Here you can see the great bulk of Traprain Law, the Bass Rock and forty miles of the Fife coastline. You pass an ancient sign for the Goblin Ha' Hotel, and now it is down, down, down.

Three kilometres short of Gifford, turn right for Garvald at a little crossroads. Carry on between manicured beech hedges, then just when you think you are back in the lowlands, a monumental little hill rears up out of a waterless valley to spoil the enjoyment, but it is the last climb. Nunraw appears across the fields and you know there is not far to go. The stream zigzags under the road and soon the white houses of Garvald appear. Was it worth it? Of course it was!

View on the way back

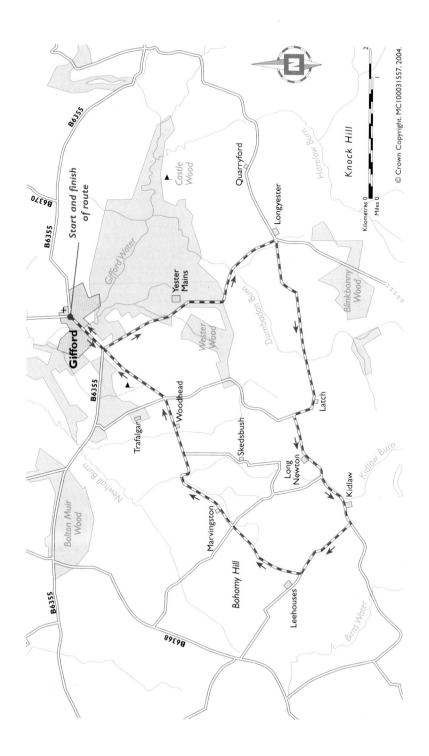

© Crown Copyright. MCI 0003 1557. 2004.

GIFFORD AND THE YESTERS

The village of Gifford was planned and built by the Marquis of Tweeddale in the early part of the eighteenth century to replace the old village of Bothans, which the Marquis considered to be too close to Yester House, his new palatial residence. This beautiful village has changed little, retaining much of its eighteenth and nineteenth-century character. It transmits a light and airy feel as soon as you arrive and it takes very little sun to light up the main street with its white buildings, shops, hotels and the impressive church. Gifford is the largest of the Lothian hill-foot villages.

Directly opposite the Mercat Cross is the start of the mile-long tree-lined avenue which leads to Yester House. The Avenue begins with a neat row of houses on one side and a large green or bleaching ground separating the other line of cottages on the other. The house, which was built by the fourth Marquis of Tweeddale in 1745, was designed first by James Smith and was later substantially modified by Robert Adam. Close to Yester House is the old Collegiate Church of St Baithen, built by the Lords of Yester in 1421, which was once the parish church of the village of Bothans. Since the demise of the village, the grounds have been used as a burial place by the Tweeddale family.

Almost a mile further east along the banks of Gifford Water lie the ruins of the old Castle of Yester, which was built by Sir Hugo de Gifford on the lands granted to him by William the Lion in 1190. The castle, built in 1267, contains a vaulted hall situated entirely below ground level. It is much larger than the normal subterranean prison built into most Scottish castles, and the reason for its construction is not known. It is known as Goblin Ha' and,

Mercat Cross, Gifford

Goblin Ha' Inn, Gifford

according to Scott's poem, *Marmion*, has links with witchcraft.

Sir Hugo was known as a wizard or hobgoblin and endowed with supernatural qualities striking fear into the local population. A gypsy acquaintance tells the tale of a New Zealander he took to visit the Ha' whose hair stood on end the moment he attempted to enter.

Depart south west on the B6355, cross the bridge over the Gifford Water, then turn south towards Longyester at the crossroads by the golf club car park. You return to this junction at the end of the ride. Immediately, your eye is drawn to the range of the Lammermuirs stretched out along the horizon, but fear not, you ride up to them, not over! This is a tour in hill country but not in the hills themselves.

Soon you enter a splendid beech avenue, which is cool in summer, then burst into open country and head for Longyester. The signpost by the burn has lost most of its letters, but you do not need to be a crossword expert to choose the correct direction. It is uphill of course!

Turn right before Longyester farm, up the last serious hill and then ride parallel to the Lammermuirs. The views open out to the north, the Laws of Traprain and Berwick, the

Hopetoun Monument, Inchkeith island in the Firth of Forth, and in the distance the Kingdom of Fife with the Lomond Hills still further. What seemed like a million crows may tumble and greet you at Pishwanton Wood. Another sustained but reasonable climb from the Dumbadan Burn takes you past Over Newton to the red and white house at West Latch. Near here there is a small road which takes you part of the way towards a series of the Iron Age forts and settlements so prevalent in this part of the country.

Signpost at Longyester

There is no signpost at the junction beyond Long Newton, so bear left at the telephone box and up past the gorse-covered hillside to Kidlaw, wonderfully perfumed and awash with colour at certain times of year. Make what you want of the next old signpost, but head right, turning your back to the Lammermuirs, and approach Leehouses, where unfortunately there is nothing to point the way apart from noisy geese and manicured beech hedges. However, take the right turn here.

Carry on to Marvingston and head straight on through to Gifford. The momentum is inter-rupted at the sharp little hill by Skedsbush Bridge and then by the most minor of inclines at Woodhead, which can be surmounted by a judicious spell of overgearing, attacking in a higher gear than normal. However, that is definitely the last climb, thereafter it is downhill all the way, past the golf course to the first crossroads on the route and onwards into Gifford.

Poppies

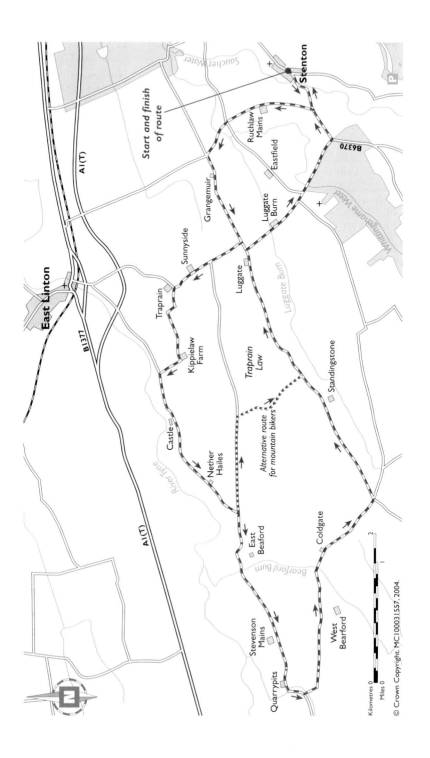

© Crown Copyright. MC100031557, 2004.

STENTON AND TRAPRAIN LAW

The great mass of Traprain Law, visible throughout much of East Lothian, is a laccolith, formed 300 million years ago by volcanic activity. Molten magma was forced upwards, causing the surface rocks to swell, and then solidified. Erosion by glaciation left the Law as an exposed basalt mound 221 metres above sea level. In the setting of the gently undulating ground around it this hill looks substantial.

Stenton (meaning 'stone town') is a picturesque agricultural village, dating back to about 1500 and designated an Outstanding Conservation Area in 1969. Most buildings are of a characteristic pink-purple sandstone unique to the area; they have orange pantile roofs and are set around a series of greens. The restored Mercat Post and Scales on the East Green are a reminder of the weekly cattle and sheep markets held here between 1681 and 1862. The Parish Church was built in 1829 by William Burn in a Gothic style, and has some fine late nineteenth century stained glass. In the churchyard there are remains of the sixteenth century Old Parish Church, including its tower, and some interesting graves.

Head south-west through the village on the B6370, over the Sauchet Water and up a steep hill for 250 m, then turn right towards the seventeenth century Ruchlaw House on the crest of the hill. Little steep hills are a feature of this route. You may, if you like, dismount and walk up, then freewheel down!

At Ruchlaw Mains carry straight on at the junction, and at the next junction, a kilometre further on, turn left towards Luggate. Travel another 1.5 km towards Luggate and turn right, following the road to East Linton for a kilometre past the impressive Sunnyside

INFORMATION

Distance: 22 km (13.75 miles). Circular route. If you choose the rough path option the route is 15.5 km (9.75 miles).

Start and finish: Parish Church car park, Stenton.

Map: OS Landranger, sheet 67, and Spokes East Lothian Cycle Map.

Terrain: Minor roads. Undulating route.

Refreshments: In Stenton only.

Old church in Stenton

Barn at Luggate

Farm. Splendid engine-house chimneys like the one at Sunnyside are a feature of East Lothian farms, reminders of the days when threshing machines were steam-driven. As you climb the hill, you gain a fine view of Traprain Law.

After Sunnyside you arrive at a three-way junction. Turn left on to a much narrower road, leading to Hailes Castle. Beyond Kippielaw the road plunges down into the Tyne valley. At the T-junction at the bottom of the hill turn left, and within 500 m you come to the castle.

Hailes Castle, one of the oldest castles in Scotland, was probably built by Hugo de Gourlay during the thirteenth century. The Gourlays lost their lands for supporting the English during the Wars of Independence and Sir Adam de Hepburn became the new lord. In 1567 James Hepburn, fourth earl of Bothwell and Mary Queen of Scots' third husband, forfeited the lands. The castle passed to the Stewarts, then to the Setons, but Cromwell's Roundheads are said to have dismantled it in 1650.Unlike many fortifications which were built high on a hill, Hailes is set in a very pleasant situation by the River Tyne, and is a good place for a break despite the sound of the traffic on the nearby A1.

When you reach the junction beyond Nether Hailes you come to a signposted cycle route. Here there are two alternative routes that can be followed.

To take the first, if you are on a mountain bike and not averse to a bit of rough riding, then turn left and carry on for 2 km to where you will see a rough path on the right. This is an interesting old road cutting across the col to the west of Traprain Law.To follow the second, which remains on-road, turn right and follow this road towards Haddington for 3 km, to the junction of the minor road signposted for

Garvald. After cycling on this for 3 km, turn left at the fourway junction and carry on for 2 km to where the rough path once again joins the road and the two alternative routes are reunited.

The rough-stuff route, which can be quite overgrown, has a stony base and quite a few brambles. The quarry face, on the north, hosts doves and a colony of fulmars.

Hailes Castle on the River Tyne

The obelisk on the hill to the south commemorates James Maitland Balfour of Whittinghame, nineteenth-century MP and Major Commandant of the East Lothian Yeomanry Cavalry.

When you are this close to the Law it is easy to understand why its commanding position attracted ancient communities. By around 1500 BC the Bronze Age population were using it for burial, then a later hill fort was probably the capital of the Gododdin tribe, known as the Votadini by the Romans. The Gododdin occupied much of south east Scotland in the later centuries BC and embraced the Roman occupation readily. A remarkable hoard of Roman silver was found here in 1919.

Now back on the road. Head east to the T-junction, where a barn has an interesting array of farm equipment attached to its walls. Here turn right and almost immediately start on the last real climb of the day. This takes you past Whittinghame House, family home of British Prime Minister Arthur Balfour (1848–1930). Then on through a long damp tunnel which turns into a narrow sunken road. At the end of this road turn left on to the B6370 and ride along to where the first hill, so arduous a climb at the outset, now offers a fast descent back into Stenton.

Traprain Law from Berwick Law

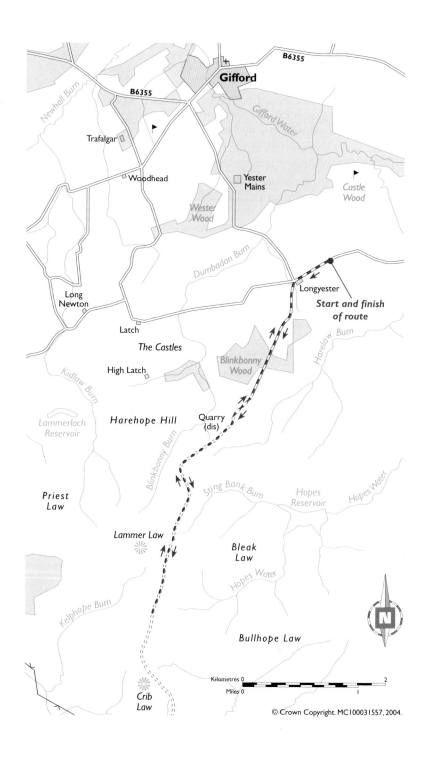

Gifford

B6355

B6355

Gifford Water

Newhall Burn

Trafalgar

Woodhead

Yester Mains

Castle Wood

Wester Wood

Dumbadan Burn

Longyester

Start and finish of route

Long Newton

Latch

Harelaw Burn

The Castles

Blinkbonny Wood

Kidlaw Burn

High Latch

Lammerloch Reservoir

Harehope Hill

Quarry (dis)

Blinkbonny Burn

Sting Bank Burn

Hopes Reservoir

Hopes Water

Priest Law

Lammer Law

Bleak Law

Hopes Water

Kelphope Burn

Bullhope Law

Crib Law

Kilometres 0   2
Miles 0   1

N

© Crown Copyright. MC100031557, 2004.

LAMMER LAW, THE HEART OF THE LAMMERMUIRS

The Lammermuir Hills form the backdrop to all the routes in East Lothian and several in Midlothian too. You may have skirted the northern slopes on earlier routes, a couple even probing a little, but this old coaching road over Lammer Law (527 m) strikes straight through their heart. It has been said that if Soutra was the gate of Lothian, then Lammer Law is the gatepost. The more obvious reason for the twentieth century development in favour of Soutra is the fact that, despite the snow gates on the A68, it is 144 m lower—a major factor in keeping the modern winter traffic moving. Today you will climb to 507 m.

Strangely, Lammer Law is not the highest hill in the range that bears its name. Meikle Says Law, about five kilometres to the east, is eight metres higher, but also lies on the Lothian border.

Although the River Tweed is often regarded as the true Scottish Border, many scholars have been of the opinion that it was actually the Lammermuir Hills that presented the last great obstacle to invading armies. Even in summer these brown acres, with steep-sided cleuchs, can be intimidating, and, short as it is, this ride should be treated with respect. The weather up on the tops can be very different to that in which you start the ride, so go prepared. Even on the brightest day take a windproof jacket.

The name Lammer is almost certainly associated with the word lamb. Sheep farming is, and always has been, the most important element of the economy in these high pastures. Throughout the Lammermuirs you will find names directly connected with sheep; Hogs Law and Hogs Rig, a hog being a yearling, Ewelairs Hill, Wedder Law, Wether Law, Wedderlie and Wedder Lair, a wedder or

INFORMATION

Distance: 11 km (6.8 miles). Linear route.

Start and finish: Hopes Road, near Longyester. Alternative start in Gifford, to approach Longyester from the north. This adds 5.0 km to the route.

Map: OS Landranger, sheet 66, and Spokes East Lothian Cycle Map.

Terrain: Minor road to begin, but the heart of the route lies over an old coaching road with an unsealed surface. Mountain bike terrain.

Refreshments: None en route, unless you use the extension to Carfrae Mill, where meals are available at the hotel.

Extensions: The coaching road runs through the Lammermuirs to Carfrae Mill, Borders Region. The return distance from Longyester to Carfrae Mill is 27.8 km (17.28 miles), of which 13.7 km (8.48 miles) is minor road. No convenient return route exists to make this a circular tour, the other crossing of the Lammermuirs in these parts being the A68 trunk road over Soutra. One solution would be to leave a vehicle at Carfrae Mill.

The trail begins

wether being a castrated ram, and of course there is Lamb Hill, Lamblair and Lamb Rig. This is most definitely sheep country.

Longyester is a large, busy farm, so the route starts nominally at the telephone box to the east. There is more room to park in the road to the Hopes, and this short extra distance will warm your legs through before you start to climb. Although this is the only true mountain bike route in the book, in the sense that some of the terrain is very uneven, a chance to get your legs moving on smoother roads before you hit the rough stuff should never be turned down. It avoids undue strain on cold muscles and gives you the opportunity to listen to your bike and confirm that all is well before other matters take precedence.

Ride west to Longyester and go straight on at the most oddly-shaped crossroads in Scotland. Even the straight on instruction is open to interpretation. The way you want is guarded by a 'No Through Road' sign, but there is an old signpost partially hidden in the trees. It is worth a look. In non-decimal figures the relevant arm reads:

Lammerlaw 2.75 miles
Carfrae Mill 8.5 miles
Lauder 12.25 miles
Impassable for motors

Thistles

—But irresistible for mountain bikers, absolutely irresistible.

The farm cottages usually have a fine collection of all-terrain vehicles outside, from a venerable, but obviously still hard-working, Ferguson tractor, through a rare Nomad pickup probably built from a kit using Mini parts, to the current shepherds' workhorse, the inevitable quad bike.

You can tell this is harsh countryside by the permanent corrugated-iron lambing pens, supplemented by the usual straw bale windbreaks at the relevant time of year, but the shepherd is obviously well used to lambing storms of some severity in April and May. The tarmac ends at a hazardous one-hinged gate, but the navigational decision is easy. It is up, on the rough.

Signpost points the way to the hills

Take note of the track. Some of the old road is firm and compacted, some of it is loose. Choose the smoothest, and probably the easiest route, weaving across from side to side if necessary and trying to remember the best line for the return journey, when you will be going a lot faster. You will forget of course, but what this will achieve is to draw your attention to the fact that there is considerable variation in different parts of this one track, and some good smooth lines do exist. Always search for the best.

Heather-burning is evident all the way up the climb. Grouse need young tender shoots to eat, and burning is one way of ensuring that. A well-managed moor will look like a patchwork quilt, with a mixture of young and mature heather: the youngest for food, the oldest for nesting cover.

After all the initial toil, over the brow of the hill the road drops into the bowl at the head of the Harelaw Burn. This is not unusual, although never popular, on moorland routes, but there is the reassurance of seeing the road climbing the side of Harehope Hill in front of you! Do not veer left towards the corrugated shed—even though the track seems slightly smoother, it only lasts 200 metres.

The line of your road can be seen sweeping left immediately above the grassy slopes at the head of the bowl, the dividing line between

Look back to the Bass Rock

pasture and moor. The road becomes compacted grass in places, which can be quite hazardous when descending in wet conditions, so take note of the grassy patches. There is a brief glimpse of the star-shaped Hopes Reservoir before it becomes hidden again among the cleuchs.

If you have saved this route until last you will see many of the salient features of other routes when you pause as you climb—Traprain Law, North Berwick Law, Bass Rock, the Hopetoun Monument beyond Haddington and the Firth of Forth. Do your sightseeing on the way up, as you will need all your concentration on the way down. Then, quite suddenly, between the gates, the road starts to descend again. You have reached the top. The Lothian border sits on the col beyond the second gate, at the track junction. This is the turnaround point, unless you are pressing on to Carfrae Mill, which is reached by simply following the main track, so retrace your route to the last gate and reap the rewards of your labours with a splendid ride back down.

Make sure your helmet is properly secured and do not get carried away on the descent. The major part of the braking should be done with your back brake without skidding, but you will need a lot of front brake too, which actually does most of the work. Never lock the front brake, because you will lose steerage, and do not forget there is a gate at the bottom!

INDEX